SNOWDONIA
NATIONAL PARK

SNOWDONIA
NATIONAL PARK

Showell Styles

MICHAEL JOSEPH

Acknowledgements
For help in the preparation of the text and illustrations in
this book the author's thanks are due to the following:

The staff of the Snowdonia National Park Authority
The staff of the Countryside Commission
Philip Evans
Eileen Clayton
E Breeze Jones
Dr John Llywelyn Williams.

New photographs taken for the Countryside
Commission by Philip Evans.
Wildlife photographs on pages 89, 92, 93, 97, 100
and 105 kindly supplied by E. Breeze Jones and those
on page 87 by Eileen Clayton.

First published in Great Britain 1987 by
Webb & Bower (Publishers) Limited
9 Colleton Crescent, Exeter, Devon EX2 4BY
in association with Michael Joseph Limited
27 Wright's Lane, London W8 5SL
and The Countryside Commission,
John Dower House, Crescent Place,
Cheltenham, Glos GL50 3RA

Designed by Ron Pickless

Production by Nick Facer/Rob Kendrew

Illustrations by Rosamund Gendle/Ralph Stobart

Text and new photographs Copyright © The Countryside Commission
Illustrations Copyright © Webb & Bower (Publishers) Ltd

British Library Cataloguing in Publication Data
The National parks of Britain.
Snowdonia
1.   National parks and reserves — England —
Guide-books   2.   England — Description and
travel — 1971-   — Guide-books.
I.   Styles, Showell, *1908–*
914.2′04858   SB484.G7.

ISBN 0–86350–337–0

Typeset in Great Britain by Keyspools Ltd., Golborne, Lancs.

Printed and bound in Hong Kong by Mandarin Offset.

Contents

Preface

Snowdonia is one of ten national parks which were established in the 1950s. These largely upland and coastal areas represent the finest landscapes in England and Wales and present us all with opportunities to savour breathtaking scenery, to take part in invigorating outdoor activities, to experience rural community life, and most importantly, to relax in peaceful surroundings.

The designation of national parks is the product of those who had the vision, more than fifty years ago, to see that ways were found to ensure that the best of our countryside should be recognized and protected, that the way of life therein should be sustained, and that public access for open-air recreation should be encouraged.

As the government planned Britain's post-war reconstruction, John Dower, architect, rambler and national park enthusiast, was asked to report on how the national park ideal adopted in other countries could work for England and Wales. An important consideration was the ownership of land within the parks. Unlike other countries where large tracts of land are in public ownership, and thus national parks can be owned by the nation, here in Britain most of the land within the national parks was, and still is, privately owned. John Dower's report was published in 1945 and its recommendations accepted. Two years later another report drafted by a committee chaired by Sir Arthur Hobhouse proposed an administrative system for the parks, and this was embodied in the National Parks and Access to the Countryside Act 1949.

This Act set up the National Parks Commission to designate national parks and advise on their administration. In 1968 the National Parks Commission became the Countryside Commission but we continue to have national responsibility for our national parks which are administered by local government, either through committees of the county councils or independent planning boards.

This guide to the landscape, settlements and natural history of Snowdonia National Park is one of a series on all ten parks. As well as helping the visitor appreciate the park and its attractions, the guides outline the achievements of and pressures facing the national park authorities today.

Our national parks are a vital asset, and we all have a duty to care for and conserve them. Learning about the parks and their value to us all is a crucial step in creating more awareness of the importance of the national parks so that each of us can play our part in seeing that they are protected for all to enjoy.

Sir Derek Barber
Chairman
Countryside Commission

Introduction

The Snowdon massif from the north east. The sharp horns of Crib Goch, left, begin the long narrow ridge which stretches to Carnedd Ugain, on the right. Thence a broader saddle gives easy walking to Yr Wyddfa (Snowdon summit) seen beyond.

Within the age-old boundaries of Wales there exists a land so compact and homogeneous, so different from its neighbouring territories, that for seven centuries it was a separate kingdom. The royal princes of Gwynedd claimed equality with the Anglo-Norman kings of England, and one of them, Llywelyn the Great, married the daughter of King John. When Llywelyn, no doubt wishing to impress his father-in-law on this occasion, assumed a new title he named himself Dominus Snaudoniae, Lord of Snowdonia. This was in the year 1230, so the name 'Snowdonia' has long-standing historical warrant.

The kingdom of Gwynedd consisted almost wholly of mountains, wild and rugged ranges from Cadair Idris (Giant Idris's Chair) at its southern limit to Eryri (Abode of Eagles) in the north. The early mariners gazing across the wintry waves of the Irish

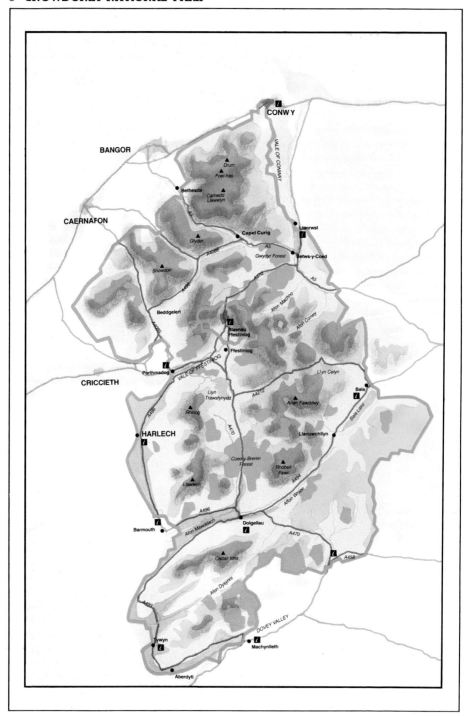

The Snowdonia National Park.

Sea to the white-capped mountains of Eryri called them Snaudune, the Snowy Hills; a name which later visitors were to attach to the highest mountain of them all, Snowdon. Beyond the mountains in the north west lay the flatter and more fertile lands whose harvests and herds supplied Gwynedd: the peninsula of Lleyn and the island of Môn or Anglesey, both quite different in character from the rest of the kingdom. When the old Welsh kingdoms were carved into new shires after the Act of Union in 1536, Gwynedd became the two shires of Caernarfon and Meirionnydd with Anglesey a third shire; recent revision has put Gwynedd back on the map in its rightful place. But through all the changes time has brought – of county boundaries, roads and railways, industrial development – the mountains of Gwynedd have retained their character as a region of wild natural beauty, a kingdom apart still and ruled over by that prince of mountains, Snowdon. When a wise generation decided that this character must be preserved the region became Snowdonia National Park.

The park was designated in 1951, the second largest of the ten national parks of England and Wales. For boundaries it has the waters of Cardigan Bay on the west and the River Dyfi and its estuary on the south; on the east the boundary line follows the Conwy Valley, then on southward to the eastern end of Bala lake where it links with the upper stream of the Dyfi. The northern boundary, having cut across the base of the Lleyn Peninsula and the region near the Menai Strait, runs slightly inland of the coast of Conwy Bay as far as Conwy. This boundary line excludes areas that have been partly industrialized like the quarry regions of Llanberis and Bethesda north of Snowdon, and a circular area of some ten square miles embracing the slate-quarried hills of Blaenau Ffestiniog is also excluded from the park. Such exclusions, of course, don't imply that these regions have nothing of interest for the visitor. Some of them have great interest for the industrial archaeologist and even for the lover of the picturesque. But Snowdonia was designated a national park because of its scenic natural beauty, the preservation of which was considered to be of great national importance; and where past or present industrial activities have made conservation impracticable it would obviously be foolish to attempt it.

The unspoiled beauty of the park, then, covers an area of 840 square miles. Imagine a rough diamond-

A park information board by the Mymbyr lakes at Capel Curig.

Tryfan (3,010 ft, 918 m) from Llyn Caseg Fraith. Offering climbing and scrambling of all grades, Tryfan is said to be the one mountain of Snowdonia which cannot be climbed without using one's hands.

shape of that size, with two scratches running across it at equal intervals on a downward slant from right to left, and you have a very rough plan of its layout. The scratches represent the troughs of river valleys reaching the Cardigan Bay coast in wide estuaries at Porthmadog and at Barmouth farther south; a third river and estuary, the Dyfi, shapes the southern tip of the diamond. Between these lines are the mountain masses each with its own intricate topography of pass and river valley and outlying spur: Snowdon and Glyder and Carnedd north of the top line, Rhinog and Arenig in the middle, Cadair Idris and its dependency, the Aran, in the south. This division of the land into groups of mountains may seem to ignore other features but in fact it does not, for in Snowdonia National Park it is the mountains that ordain what the other features shall be and where they shall appear. Their 'cwms' – Welsh for cirques, or coombs – and ridges shape the hill farms, their valleys guide the roads and establish the positions of villages and towns, their rivers widening down to the coast decide where ports and harbours and seaside resorts shall be located. My three divisions wouldn't please a geologist, who would object that a lot of quite

Snowdon from the south east. The Watkin path mounts the wide glen of Cwm Llan, seen here, by way of Bwlch y Saethau, where tradition places the site of King Arthur's last battle.

disparate rocks are lumped together in the northern division. But – for me at least – the three groups signify three districts, each of which has a different character from the others.

Living as I have done for forty years on the border between Caernarfon and Meirionnydd (my northern and middle divisions), I've savoured and enjoyed this difference on innumerable occasions. Heading north for a day's walk or scramble, I enter a region that has the grandeur and the dark glamour of the Gothic. Spiky summits and knife-edge ridges soar above deep-sunken valleys where the last remnants of the centuries-old forests linger by the shores of the lakes. Standing 3,560 ft (1,085 m) up on the summit of Snowdon (SH 609543), highest top of England and Wales, you feel these bristling mountains as the impregnable fortress they once were, the last stronghold of warriors. Even the hotel and the Snowdon Mountain Railway can't make you forget that you are standing on Yr Wyddfa Fawr, the Great Tumulus, where the giant Rhita (who wore a robe made of Saxon beards) lies buried; or that the two Carneddau summits in the northern distance were named Llewelyn and Dafydd after two warlike princes. The atmosphere of these mountains north

Dinas Cromlech, a popular rock-climbing face in Llanberis Pass, is well seen from the A4086 road.

of the Glaslyn is strenuous, stirring, as sharp and exciting as their rocks.

If I go southward into the middle division I go into northern Meirionnydd and into a quite different atmosphere. Here the long lonely pastures of the ancient land of Ardudwy slant down to the sea, a countryside redolent of timeless peace. All the hill slopes are littered with the remains of past cultures and lifestyles from prehistoric to more modern times. Standing stones and cromlechs, the ruins high on the moors of dwellings where the earliest hill farmers lived, the seventeenth-century mansion of Cors-y-gedol (SH 598231), drovers' roads and medieval trading routes, ancient chapels like those at Llandecwyn and Llandanwg and Llanaber – all these add to the impression of a land inhabited and domesticated since very early times. There hangs above the upland farms and the streams that whisper in the high moorland an air of nostalgia, the feeling the Welsh call *hiraeth*. The mountains have played their part in forming this land. Standing well back from the coast, the fourteen-mile-long barrier of the Rhinog defends it on the east and only allows difficult access through the dramatic cleft of the Bwlch Drws Ardudwy, the Door of Ardudwy, between Rhinog Fawr and Rhinog Fach (SH 660283). Beyond that Door a wide tract of marsh and forest, holding Trawsfynydd with its power station and lake, reaches away eastward to twin-summited Arenig and the park boundary at Bala. The Rhinog ridge, wildest and roughest of all Welsh mountain regions, continues southward in the lofty humps of the Llawlechs to end craggily at Barmouth, old port and modern seaside holiday resort. And here the

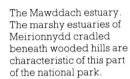

The Mawddach estuary. The marshy estuaries of Meirionnydd cradled beneath wooded hills are characteristic of this part of the national park.

wide Mawddach estuary, running inland for seven miles to Dolgellau, makes the lovely northern boundary of my third and southernmost region.

Cadair Idris dominates all this region. The long north-facing wall of its precipices above Dolgellau is one of the great sights of the park, and the north-eastern extension of its ridge, broken only by two high road-passes, reaches by way of the two Aran summits right from the sea coast to Llyn Tegid, Bala lake. While the Rhinog mountains of my middle section are constructed of the ancient Cambrian rocks, Cadair itself is made of the same igneous rock as Snowdon; and yet I find when I cross the Mawddach that I have once again entered another countryside with its own individual atmosphere. The bright open vales of Dysinni and Fathew and the tangled woodland dells that fall to the Mawddach shores are characteristic of south Meirionnydd, subtly different from the vales and dells of the north, and Snowdon – ten miles from the sea – has nothing resembling those lofty hill-crests that roll down from Cadair to the coast at Tywyn and Llwyngwril. When you come over the hill ridges south of the Dysinni river and look down on the Dyfi Valley and the southern boundary of the park, you perceive that you have reached a frontier. South of the Dyfi a wilderness of rounded hills and high moorlands stretches for fifty miles, a countryside with charms of its own but lacking the variety and boldness of scenery to be found within Snowdonia National Park.

Immense variety in small compass is to my mind the greatest attribute of this park. Consider, for instance, the range of ecologies presenting

Llyn Dinas, under the eastern flank of Snowdon. A public footpath follows the shores of the lake.

themselves between dune lands at sea level and mountain crests more than 3,000 ft (914 m) higher – the birds and beasts and plants of estuary, meadow, woodland, high pasture, moorland, crag. Or the compactness that allows one to take a morning dip in the sea, climb a mountain in the afternoon, and watch a nuthatch pottering round the bole of a forest tree in the afternoon. One Easter day I was cutting steps in the snow-ice of a mountain gully at noon and four hours later having a picnic tea on the beach with my family; there can be very few other places in the world where that is possible. And besides climbing and sea-bathing and bird-watching there are many other things to be enjoyed in Snowdonia, for the second statutory requirement of the National Park Authority is to provide facilities for the enjoyment of open-air recreation. Many organizations have taken advantage of these facilities, so that there are (among other interests) nature trails, canoeing, industrial archaeology, camp sites, sailing, and various museums and working examples of the traditional crafts of the area. Perhaps the hill walker is the most fortunate beneficiary, with a network of paths and rights of way at his feet. In addition to its multitude of mountains the park contains more than 150 lakes; a walker setting out to visit all the lakes of Snowdonia would lay up an incomparable store of memorable scenes and experiences. As for the rock climber, he has dozens of famous rock-faces to choose from and Plas-y-Brenin, the National Centre for Mountain Activities at Capel Curig (SH 717578), to go to for instruction in his craft. And for walker and climber and all who venture away from the public roads and tracks there is one very important thing to be remembered.

Strictly speaking, Snowdonia National Park is neither 'national' nor a 'park'. Less than twenty-five per cent of the land is owned or managed by the National Trust, the National Park Authority, the Water Authority, and the Forestry Commission. All the rest – three-quarters of the park – is privately owned or managed by farmers. Ample access by public footpaths or rights of way is provided and marked on the map (the current Ordnance Survey Outdoor Leisure maps of the area are the best), but away from these you walk the hills by courtesy of the farmers whose pastures they are. It's only reasonable to expect that in return you will avoid damaging walls, leaving gates open, or – especially

A Forestry Commission picnic site. Such sites usually have an adjacent car park and access to forestry trails.

in the lambing season – taking a dog on the hills off lead, any of which could seriously endanger his stock.

The land owned by the Forestry Commission amounts to just over twelve per cent of the park. The conifer forests have their own special interest, and the Commission has provided excellent public access, nature trails, picnic sites, and information centres. Of the four forests, the Gwydyr Forest (SH 780580) (centre Betws-y-Coed) is probably the most popular, and the Arboretum provides the means of identifying the trees – no less than forty-eight different kinds! – to be found in the forests.

In addition to mountain and forest land there are about twenty-five miles of coastline within the national park. This is all on the west and most of it is wild or semi-wild and unspoilt, with its special plant life and bird life as bonuses to the pleasures of sea-bathing and sunbathing. Behind the two-mile sweep of the sandy beach at Harlech, for example, is the Morfa Harlech National Nature Reserve (SH 560340), 1,214 acres of dunes and marshland, and a few miles south of it the smaller Morfa Dyffryn Reserve (SH 560250). A permit for routes off the agreed rights of way in these reserves is needed and can be obtained from the Nature Conservancy Council office in Bangor. Sandy beaches are the rule all along this coast, where Harlech, Barmouth, Tywyn and Aberdyfi are the chief seaside resorts with all the usual facilities for bathing, boating, sailing, sail-boarding and fishing. The nature reserves just mentioned are two of the sixteen national nature reserves within the boundaries of Snowdonia Park, four of the others being mountain and the rest woodland. As a general rule, access to the mountain reserves is open and to the woodland reserves limited.

Ordnance Survey map references are given in the text for the sites and facilities mentioned, together with many others which will be found listed at the end of this book. Here also are listed the National Park Information Centres, of which there are six placed at strategic points throughout the park. At these centres you can pick up such useful things as leaflets describing the various paths up Snowdon and easier walks, the current programmes of Guided Walks and Heritage Walks, and the Talks Programme of evening slide shows, besides maps and local guide-books. The Visitor Centre at Betws-y-Coed is the largest of them, with a spacious exhibition area, an audio-visual theatre and lecture-room. Information boards, usually placed at a car park adjacent to a popular walking area, show a map of the area with routes and footpaths marked and also information about the locality.

Special mention must be made of Plas Tan-y-Bwlch, a big eighteenth-century manor house splendidly situated in the heart of the national park

The outlook from the terrace at Plas Tan-y-Bwlch, in the Vale of Ffestiniog.

at Maentwrog (SH 655406). Once the home of a wealthy family, it was acquired by the National Park Authority and converted into a residential centre for the teaching of a very wide range of environmental-based subjects. The courses here vary in length from three to seven days, and from the current list of thirty-nine courses three chosen at random will give some idea of the range – Walking in Snowdonia for Senior Citizens, Birdwatching Weekend, Landscape Painting.

Outside the area of the park but easily accessible from it are four areas of outstanding natural beauty designated by the Countryside Commission: Bardsey Island, part of the Anglesey coast, Ynys Llanddwyn (where there is also a nature reserve) and part of the coast of the Lleyn Peninsula. To reach the other two national parks in Wales would need a longer journey. The Brecon Beacons National Park and the Pembrokeshire Coast National Park each have a character of their own, a type of natural beauty quite different from that of Snowdonia. Both should be visited. But few people have leisure enough to enjoy more than one national park at a time, and a normal holiday is far too short to see all that Snowdonia has to offer.

And the weather? That is as varied as everything else within this park. Mountains proverbially make their own weather, with quick changes from sunshine to mist; and in spring and autumn, as well as in winter, frost or snow can make normally harmless slopes dangerous. It should not be necessary nowadays to emphasize that proper equipment is needed for mountains whatever the weather. A detailed weather forecast of mountain weather conditions in Snowdonia National Park can be obtained by dialling Llanberis (0286) 870120. Snowdon summit is one of the four wettest places in Britain, averaging 200 in (5,000 mm) in a year; yet the coast at Morfa Harlech ten miles away is within the belt of 'below average' rainfall. The best chance of dry weather is in May, June, and September, August being usually – but not always – a wet month. But the interest of this park is not wholly dependent on weather or season.

For among the ten national parks Snowdonia is unique in one special respect: most of the 25,000 people who live and work within the boundaries of the park are Welsh, and speak Welsh as their normal everyday language. As well as their language they have preserved a national culture

The footpath to Llyn Cau, below Cadair Idris to the south. In winter it is essential to be equipped with proper mountain gear for such walks.

and much of their traditional way of life. In conserving the scenic beauty of the region – that is, in opposing the proliferation of power stations and mining enterprises and other ugly intrusions – the National Park Authority has also been able to conserve something of this way of life, so that an observant visitor coming into the park from England will at once perceive a difference. The most obvious sign of it will be the public notices such as road signs, which are in Welsh as well as in English, and the smaller green signs which have 'public footpath' on one side and *'llwybr cyhoeddus'* – the Welsh equivalent – on the other. But there is a more subtle difference which, over the centuries, many visitors to Wales have felt and commented on; a difference of atmosphere difficult to define, depending not only on fine scenery and pure air but also on a human continuity of culture – a spell, as it were, woven long ago and still persistent in the quiet valleys under the mountains. The English poet Gerard Manley Hopkins felt it when he wrote:

'Lovely the woods, waters, meadows, cwms, vales,
All the air things wear that build this world of Wales.'

That special 'air' is something worth preserving. And the establishment of Snowdonia National Park has given it a good chance of survival.

1 The making of the landscape

From the topmost point of Yr Wyddfa Fawr, the summit of Snowdon, you can overlook the whole landscape of Snowdonia National Park: from the Carneddau mountains in the north to Cadair Idris in the south, from the sea coast that bounds it on the west to the peaks of Aran and Arenig in the east. In between are the deep valleys with their lakes, half-seen below the crowding mountains – ninety-six individual tops over 1,970 ft (600 m), according to a recent survey. All this is the result of a sequence of colossal natural activities which began hundreds of millions of years ago and are still going on.

New methods of research are causing geologists and geomorphologists to revise some previously held theories concerning the nature and sequence of these natural changes. And it is as well at this point to enter a *caveat*. Interpreting the landforms of Wales, Professor David Thomas has written recently, is 'a subject so contentious that a simple non-technical account would prove meaningless and, worse, misleading'. With that warning in mind, readers who wish to go more deeply into the intricacies of the subject are recommended to obtain the booklet, *Snowdonia National Park Scenery*, published in 1977 by the National Museum of Wales.

Radioactive dating has now established the age of the Earth at about 4,600 million years. The rocks and scenery of Snowdonia National Park record parts of the last 600 million years of this story, though from examination of the radioactive decay of uranium and thorium it is possible to say that there are rocks more than 1,500 million years old. The last part of this unimaginable period can be split into geological eras, and even for these you can fairly say 'give or take a few million years'. The oldest rocks to be found within the national park, known as the Cambrian rocks, began to be laid down as sediments something like 600 million years ago and the youngest, here mainly the Silurian, about 200 million years later; with that statement we may leave the time-scale and look at the making of the rocks.

Land and sea changed places many times during

the era of rock formation and much of the action occurred under water. Layers of tiny fragments, sediment, were deposited on the sea floor to form horizontal beds, stratum upon stratum of different materials and different thicknesses. One band of deposit, known as Pre-Cambrian, had a thickness of about 150,000 feet, and the rocks that were eventually formed from it may be seen at one or two places just outside the national park, notably in the cliffs near the South Stack lighthouse near Holyhead. On top of this another layer was deposited, the Cambrian, whose rocks can be seen in the Rhinog mountains in the centre of the park. The next system to be laid down, called the Ordovician, lay on the sea floor during the thirty million years of the Silurian deposits, which are the last with which we are concerned in considering the rocks of the national park. These diverse beds of sediment, then – Pre-Cambrian, Cambrian, Ordovician and Silurian – lay in that order in their horizontal layers. But not, by any means, in undisturbed peace.

Through all this immense period of time other great forces were at work on the Earth, heating and cooling, compressing and releasing, all at an infinitely slow speed. The Earth's crust was shifting and changing under tremendous pressures and parts of it were being submerged under the ocean and upheaved again; twice during this period the part of the Earth's surface we now call North Wales was subjected to long immersions. Towards the end of the age of the Ordovician deposits there was an increase in volcanic activity that was to have an important effect on the eventual landscape. By volcanic action is not meant the emergence of cone-shaped volcanoes belching fire and smoke. Most of it took place under water, molten rock being forced upwards to breach and penetrate the sedimentary layers, lava flows emerging to cover many square miles of the ocean floor; or a pile of volcanic ash or tuff would be pushed up high enough for its tip to form an island in the sea. These outbursts occurred at different centres and at different times, and the intrusive igneous rock was – a very long time afterwards – to display its effect in the shapes of Cadair Idris, the Aran and Arenig mountains, and Snowdon.

But at this period the sea still spread over the area and sedimentary deposits continued to be laid down for another thirty million years – the Silurian rocks, which were to be so drastically eroded that today they remain chiefly in a semicircle of hills outside

Looking up the Nant Ffrancon Pass to Glyder Fach and Y Garn. The A5 (Holyhead road) here passes through spectacular mountain scenery.

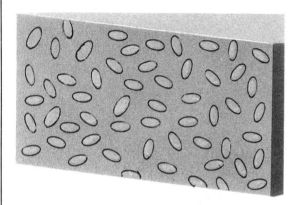

Simplified diagrams showing the formation of slaty cleavage.

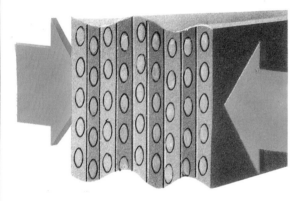

the eastern perimeter of the national park. Towards the end of the Silurian period the continents bordering the sea began moving together as a result of major movements in the earth's crust, exerting an enormous force of compression on the sequence of sedimentary layers, pushing them up into parallel folds; if you place a small hand towel on a table and slide its ends towards each other you get an idea of what happened. One movement that occurred in the region of Britain is known as the Caledonian orogeny, and its effects are seen in the way the Scottish mountains and their intervening valleys are arranged in folds and ridges running from north east to south west.

Slate rock, one day to have a special influence on Snowdonia's landscape, was formed in this era of gigantic pressures. The sedimentary mudstones and shales were more susceptible to the formation of the structure called 'slaty cleavage' than other rocks, and the exceedingly high temperatures changed their very constituency. Pressure and temperature combined to rearrange the infinitesimal particles composing them so that their usually elongated form disposed at random took on a new arrangement, with the particles compressed so that the longer axis was at right-angles to the direction of pressure. The diagram shows this slaty cleavage. The result was that such rocks tended to split in vertical sheets.

So, now, a mountainous land mass formed of folded strata stood above the surface of the sea. But millions of years were still to pass before the rocks that had been upheaved and folded bore any resemblance to the mountains we see today in Snowdonia National Park.

These striated slabs in Cwm Nantcol, near Llanbedr, show plainly the marks left by the passage of a glacier.

Erosion, the action of many forces breaking and wearing away the Earth's surface, had been at work all through the geological ages and is still at work today. You can see it happening. A frost-loosened rock falls from a crag; a mountain torrent in flood spreads an increasing fan of stones; a gale of wind

and rain scours particles from an exposed ridge.
Insignificant on the face of it; but multiply by a
million years and imagine what the mountains, or
what's left of them, will look like then. Their rocks
are all the time decaying, and will continue to decay
until the whole of Snowdonia is reduced to a plain,
its remains spread out as sand and mud on the
bottom of the sea. Erosion had begun when the land
mass rose above the sea after its first submersion,
and now, when the rock folds were finally exposed
to the atmosphere, it went on with its work. Frost,
the main operator, split the rocks, rain washed loose
material away, wind etched out weak places by
hurling particles against them, rivers moved the
loosened material from high ground to low. One
important effect of this prolonged weathering was
the depositing of a soil mantle formed from finely
ground rock containing dissolved minerals on the
slopes and in the troughs, on which plant life would
eventually find root-hold and food. Much of this
eating-away and redistribution had been done by
the time the Ice Ages arrived.

With the Ice Ages we reach what a geologist
would call very recent times. Ice spread over
Britain something like 80,000 years ago and
remained – with recessions and returns – for 70,000
years. Glaciers, fed by snowfalls that consolidated
into ice, moved slowly downward towards sea level
as accumulated weight brought the force of gravity
into play. Their action, though it did not greatly
change the basic masses of the landscape already
formed, added as it were the final dramatic touches.
The softer rocks of the rising or domelike folds – the
synclines – had gone, leaving the uneven spikes and
ridges of harder rock upstanding, and the rivers
had been at work carving away the bottoms of the
troughs or synclines. What the glaciers did was to
grind away more rock and scrape the 'V'-shaped
river-valleys into 'U'-shapes. In doing so they
created some of the most spectacular scenery in the
national park.

The hill walker can see from the mountain crests
how the ice shaped these upper ridges. On Cadair
Idris, for instance, the top of the mountain is a quite
narrow ridge separating two deep hollows
containing Llyn y Gadair (SH 708135) on one side
and Llyn Cau (SH 715215) on the other; both hollows
were gouged out by moving ice, and Llyn Cau has
been described as the most perfect glacial cirque in
Britain. Farther north among the mountains round
Snowdon there is hardly one whose flanks have not

Llŷn Idwal at the foot of Y Garn. Cwm Idwal, which contains striking glacial scenery, is at the inner (hidden) end of the lake. The easy path by which it is reached can be seen in the lower right quarter of the picture.

been carved by ice into cup-shaped bowls, cirques or (to use the Welsh name) cwms, and below the peak of Yr Wyddfa itself five major cwms, with several minor ones, demonstrate the erosive power of ice accumulations. One of the best places to see the striking scenery created by erosion and glaciation is Cwm Dyli (SH 635545), accessible by an easy two-mile walk from the car park at the top of Llanberis Pass. If you descend the Rhyd-ddu path on the other side of the mountain you have in front of you another impressive testimonial to glacial power. Across the valley is the gap of Bwlch Gylfin between Mynydd Mawr and the Nantlle Y Garn, irresistibly suggesting a gateway leading out of the mountains to the western sea; and a gateway it is, opened (according to a famous geomorphologist) by a glacier moving down from Snowdon. The mountains on either side of the gap were once joined in a continuous ridge, and the ice broke through, clearing a glacial passage for itself down the Nantlle Valley.

The gouging work of a glacier is rendered more effective by rocks embedded in its underside. When the infinitely slow progress of the Snowdonian glaciers took them down the river-

Glacier scree on Bwlch Moch, Snowdon. Evidence of the great age of Snowdonia's mountains lies everywhere under foot.

carved valleys these under-teeth scraped and smoothed the valley sides into the characteristic 'U'-shape of glacial valleys, as can be seen in Llanberis Pass and also in the Nant Ffrancon Valley (SH 640620) that runs up from Bethesda to Ogwen. Driving up the A5 road from Bethesda you see on your right hand a succession of hanging valleys, scooped out by side glaciers as they came down to join the main ice-stream in the lower valley. Besides the rocks in their undersides, the glaciers also carried down quantities of fallen rock debris on their surfaces, especially along their sides. When at last the ice retreated, melted, and vanished these huge banks of debris (moraines) were left. They can be seen in many valleys but best of all, perhaps, in Cwm Idwal under the northern flank of the Glyder range.

Cwm Idwal (SH 645595), the first national nature reserve to be established in Wales, is the most easily accessible mountain cwm in Britain. From the car park by the Ogwen Cottage Mountain School, on the A5 six miles from Bethesda, a footpath, rough but easy enough even for children, takes you in half a mile to the entrance of the reserve. Here beyond Llyn Idwal, a typical glacial lake, the great rock wall shows very clearly the folds of the strata, and the cleft known as Twll Du or the Devil's Kitchen marks the bottom of a syncline. The action of accumulating ice hollowed out this fine cirque, and when it melted at the end of the Ice Age its moraines were left as the big rounded mounds that are very obvious on the west side of the lake. On the slabby rocks in this cwm you can see the long furrows (striations) ploughed by the rocks in the glacier's underside as it ground its way outward. With so much glacial evidence to be seen in Cwm Idwal it's odd to note that when Charles Darwin first visited the Cwm with Professor Sedgwick in 1831 neither he nor his companion recognized it for what it was.

So the glaciers, having finished their sculptural task, melted with the coming of a more temperate climate and the Ice Age passed. At its passing, about 10,000 years ago, the mountains of North Wales looked very much as they look today. Hundreds of centuries of erosion had removed vast quantities of material from the upper surfaces of the folded strata and what remained was an irregular collection of ridges and lumps. In effect, the single huge syncline that had covered the area which was to become Snowdonia National Park had had its crown sheared

The still waters of Llyn Idwal occupy the bed of a glacier that was moving down Cwm Idwal 10,000 years ago.

off so that the older rocks in the centre had become exposed.

The diagram overleaf, which is simplified for the sake of clarity, must be regarded as purely diagrammatic; the indicated surfaces were not symmetrical as shown but already much cracked and eroded before the final upheaval.

The top layer, the Silurian rocks, had all been

eroded in this area, and what remained of the Ordovician survived chiefly because of the intrusions of hard igneous rock that had occurred during the period of volcanic activity. The next layer down, the Cambrian, had arched in a massive dome, now called by geologists the Harlech Dome, over the central part of the region; but all that was left of this was the group of mountains later to be named the Rhinog. As for the Pre-Cambrian, the oldest rocks, erosion had left their folded strata deep under the other layers except in the north west, outside the boundary of the present national park, where in one or two places the upper rocks had been worn away to expose them; they are to be seen on Anglesey and on the Lleyn Peninsula, and at the seaward end of Llyn Padarn (SH 580605) near Llanberis.

Simplified diagram showing geological folding and erosion in Snowdonia.

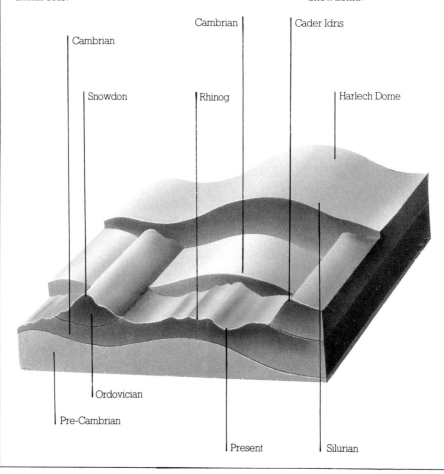

Nothing had stopped, nothing was finished. The erosive processes were, and are, still going on. But in the formation of Snowdonia's landscape the mountains were now established, though other aspects of that landscape were still to undergo changes. Many thousands of years were to pass before the mountains were given their names; but this will be a good place to skip forward in time and use their present names in a brief account of their present-day characteristics.

In the north of Snowdonia National Park, their foothills rising quite abruptly from the coast, the Carneddau mountains stand between the Conwy Valley on the east and the Nant Ffrancon Valley on the west. In form they are an eight-mile-long undulating grassy ridge running north to south, with branch ridges diverging on both sides and lakes in

Mist-wreaths hiding the valleys and roads renew the primeval landscape among the upper crags of the Glyder mountains.

the deep hollows on the east. Seven of the summits in this group are over 3,000 feet above the sea: Carnedd Llewelyn (SH 684644), Carnedd Dafydd (SH 663630), Pen yr Oleu Wen, Foel Grach, Yr Elen, Foel-fras, Garnedd Uchaf. The two first named are the second and third highest summits in Wales; Carnedd Llewelyn, 3,485 ft (1,064 m) and Carnedd

Dafydd, 3,423 ft (1,044 m) took their names from Welsh princes of the Middle Ages. The Carneddau provide one of the largest areas of high ground in the British Isles, and the walk along the whole ridge from Aber in the north to Llyn Ogwen can present hazards in mist and rain or in wintry conditions, even to experienced hill walkers. Less hardy souls will find motorable hill roads climbing into their lower eastern recesses from the Conwy Valley. The A5 road, mounting from the forests of Betws-y-Coed to cross the Nant Ffrancon Pass on its way to Bangor, separates the Carneddau from the next group to the south, the Glyder mountains.

Here again the basic shape is a ridge of crests, this time running east-west with the summits of Glyder Fach, 3,262 ft (994 m) and Glyder Fawr, 3,279 ft (999 m) and then bending north west round the hollow of Cwm Idwal to include Y Garn, 3,104 ft (946 m) and three lesser tops. Near its north-western end a notable mountain stands on a southward spur – Elidir Fawr, 3,030 ft (924 m) beneath whose south-west flank emerge the slates that gave rise to the vast Dinorwig quarries where now the Dinorwig Power Station is sited (SH 591603). More striking than any of these is Tryfan, 3,010 ft (917 m) which

Y Garn, 3,104 ft (947 m), overlooks Cwm Idwal and the Nant Ffrancon Pass. In the foreground are the lower rocks of the Gribin Ridge, a favourite route up or down Glyder Fach.

The trees and waterfalls of Cwm Llan, through which the Watkin path climbs to Snowdon's summit, contrast here with the grey crags of its upper section.

rises boldly as a northern spur above Llyn Ogwen (SH 665595). Travellers westward on the A5 have a superb view of this tusk of bare rock, a literally outstanding example of how the harder igneous rock survived when the softer rocks were eroded from around it. Tryfan can't be climbed without using your hands, and its east face was one of the earliest haunts of rock climbers. The Glyders, indeed, provide the rock climber with many faces of hard sound rock, and where they drop on the south west into Llanberis Pass are the crags known to climbers as the Three Cliffs where some of the severest climbing in Britain is to be found. Opposite the Three Cliffs rises the great flank of Snowdon.

Snowdon summit, 3,560 ft (1,085 m) is the hub from which radiate six ridges and five main paths of ascent; the Park Authority has produced excellent leaflets describing each of these paths, with its route marked on a sketch plan. The easiest way to the top for the ordinary walker runs up the ridge from Llanberis, which is also used by the Snowdon Mountain Railway; the narrow 'knife-edge' ridge of Crib Goch is the hardest, and if followed by descent over Y Lliwedd forms part of the Snowdon Horseshoe, one of the finest ridge-walks south of the

Scottish border. The most scenic path – a very popular one – starts from the car park on Llanberis Pass and ascends past the lakes of Llydaw and Glaslyn, passing close to the soaring east face of Y Lliwedd where famous climbers such as George Mallory made their first ascents. The Watkin path, a long-established route, comes up from a car park on the A498 in the Gwynant Valley, and from the same starting point Snowdon's south ridge can be gained and followed to the top. For a walker's ascent of Snowdon with little difficulty and exciting views I would choose the path from Rhyd-ddu on the A4085 (car park) and use for descent the Snowdon Ranger path, which comes down within easy distance of the start and permits a cautious look down the vertical crags of Clogwyn du'r Arddu where Joe Brown and others have displayed their climbing skill for the television cameras.

North west from Snowdon runs a rounded grassy ridge of which Moel Eilio, 2,382 ft (726 m) is the highest top, and on the south Yr Aran, 2,451 ft (747 m) rises from the foot of the south ridge. Westward Mynydd Mawr rises above Llyn Cwellyn and eastward the graceful peak of Moel Siabod, 2,861 ft (872 m) stands like a sentinel, its western slopes apt for winter skiiing. Between Snowdon and the sea is the horsehoe of high ridges enclosing Cwm Pennant, Mynydd Craig Cwm Silin on the seaward arm rising to 2,408 ft (734 m) and Moel Hebog, 2,566 ft (783 m) overlooking Beddgelert.

Continuing southward, we come to the Moelwyn group, between the Gwynant Valley and the Vale of Ffestiniog, with Moelwyn Mawr, 2,527 ft (770 m) the highest of seven tops over 2,000 feet. Its neighbour Cnicht, 262 ft (80 m) lower and a favourite ascent, is a very Proteus of mountains, appearing from the neighbourhood of Porthmadog as a sharp-pointed cone but from other angles showing a long, almost level, ridge or a peak with three summits.

The Rhinog mountains stretch their chain of rugged tops between Ffestiniog and the Mawddach Valley, a region of clefts and crags and tall heather very different from Snowdon's deep cwms and lofty ridges. Paths are few, the going always hard; to be lost in the mist on the Rhinog is a serious matter, even for experienced walkers. Rhinog Fawr, 2,362 ft (720 m) is the presiding genius of this wilderness, but Y Llethr, 2,475 ft (756 m) is the highest summit. At two points the mountains can be approached by car, both routes starting from the village of Llanbedr on the A496 coastal road: by the Nantcol Valley, where

The Artro River, which flows from Llyn Cwmbychan to the sea at Llanbedr, passes through unspoiled natural woodland. Among fishermen it is noted for its trout.

Carreg y Saeth, Rock of the Arrow, in Cwmbychan. Haunt of feral goats, this little mountain stands above the Cwmbychan lake and guards the wild defile of the Roman Steps.

you can continue with a rough walk into the scenic defile of the Bwlch Drws Ardudwy, and by the Cwm Bychan Valley (SH 640310), a place of rare charm with one of the most beautiful lakes in Wales.

Away to the east from the Rhinog ridge, twin-pointed Arenig Fawr, 2,801 ft (854 m) pokes its summit above the intervening moorland hills, a worthwhile ascent if you go up past Llyn Arenig Fawr from the lane south of Llyn Celyn. Bala lake (SH 910340) is beyond it on the south east, and from the end of the lake the Aran mountains begin the long south-westerly ridge which is the southern bastion of the national park. Hill walkers should note that on the Arans access is limited to certain paths which must be followed; National Park Information Centres can supply a map showing these paths. Aran Fawddwy, 2,974 ft (905 m) is the highest summit south of Snowdon, topping Cadair Idris by forty-six feet. From it the mountain barrier bends westward, dipping to two road-passes and rising again over Mynydd Moel to Penygadair, 2,928 ft (893 m), the top of Cadair Idris. The ascent of Cadair, as its devotees call this noble mountain, can be made with little difficulty by the path that starts from near Llyn Gwernan on the Dolgellau side; but the route from the other side, climbing into the splendid scenery of Cwm Cau with the grand northward view from the summit for a final breath-taker, is more satisfying though a little harder. Between Cadair Idris and the long trough of the Dyfi Valley rises a parallel mass of lower hills, forested on the slopes above the valley. And below these the north bank of the river makes the boundary of the national park.

The Mawddach River winds down through dense woodland below the picturesque Rhaeadr Mawddach before reaching its wide estuary near Dolgellau.

In this brief account of the mountain groups, innumerable lesser summits, ridges, and crags have of course been omitted. The mountain tops, though they dominate the landscape, are by no means the whole of it. And we return now through 10,000 years of time to see what was happening to the landscape below and around the high hills.

The last of the glaciers disappeared a hundred centuries ago from Snowdonia. Rain and wind, frost and snow, went on wearing away the rock and creating soil which a thousand streams and rivers carried down to the lower slopes and valleys. Some glacier-shaped valleys became filled with this silt and formed flat straths, as can be seen in the Nant Ffrancon, and in other valleys obstructing rocks dammed the outflow of the streams so that lakes were created. The rivers draining Snowdon on the south found themselves blocked by a rock barrier cutting them off from the sea and slowly carved a way through it, deepening the gorge to make what we now call the Pass of Aberglaslyn (SH 595463), a world-famous beauty spot. The fine-ground material they had carried down was deposited on the sea floor of the wide coastal inlet beyond. A very long time afterwards (in the nineteenth century of man's

Ancient woodland of oak and birch still remain in some places, as here on the shore of Llyn Cynwch.

reckoning) a mile-long dam reclaimed this spread of fertile deposit from the sea, giving the 10,000 acres of level farm land on the *traeth* inland of Porthmadog.

All this downward-carrying of soil material meant that the high ground was left with only the thinnest covering below the emergent rocks of the crests, while the lower slopes and valleys were provided with the means of supporting plant life. And plant life arrived, grew, and thrived. Some time in the period succeeding the end of the Ice Age the climate of Britain became warmer and drier than it has ever been since, encouraging the growth of woodlands on the slopes as high as 2,000 feet above the sea. These conditions persisted until about 3,000 years ago, when the wetter and cooler climate we know today began to set in. Trees, especially birches, clothed the Welsh hills and the lower mountains, and you can sometimes see their remains in the high peaty moorland that took the place of these woodlands. When the trees could no longer live on the high uplands they retreated to the more favourable height of about 1,000 feet; and from there down to sea level, all over Snowdonia, they flourished and spread into dense forest.

The mountains, lakes and rivers of Snowdonia.

Area covered by National Park

Principal towns ●

Plas Tan-y-Bwlch

National Nature Reserves ■

Principal summits ▲

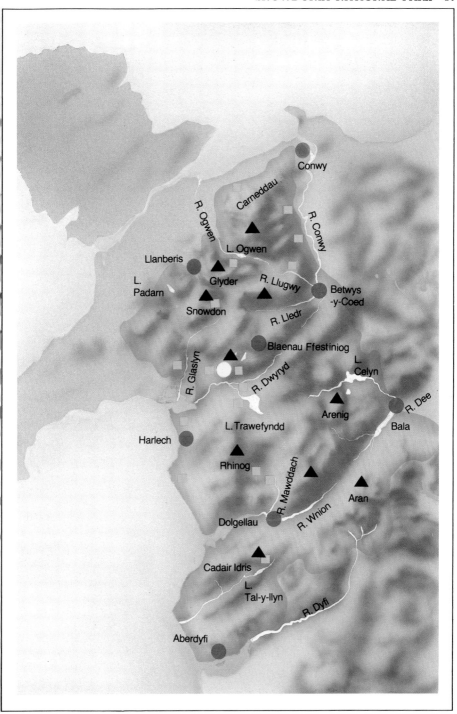

Today hardly anything is left of this great lower forest, which consisted largely of sessile oaks. Small sections of the original woodlands have been protected, just in time, as nature reserves in the national park; Coed Rhygen is a good example of what the Snowdonian forest of thirty centuries ago looked like, and you can see it by taking a lane that leaves the A470 near Trawsfynydd and follows the west side of Trawsfynydd lake. Easier to get at are the Maentwrog woodlands, Coed Camlyn and Coed Cymerau, close to the study centre at Plas Tan-y-Bwlch.

The forest was the last of nature's additions to the landscape. But almost simultaneously with its creation there appeared a new agency which was to take a hand in changing it yet again. Little by little over the years between 3000 BC and the present day this vast deciduous forest, which once covered the lower lands of Snowdonia National Park and lapped far up its mountain sides, disappeared. The agency chiefly responsible for its disappearance was humankind.

2 Early man in Snowdonia

In 1981 human remains dated to 200,000 years ago were discovered at Pontnewydd cave in North Wales, and there is evidence that *homo sapiens*, who was colonizing Europe from about 35,000 years ago, was present in association with Upper Paleolithic stone assemblages in the Vale of Clwyd. With the final withdrawal and melting of the Snowdonian Ice Cap the area would have been open for colonization by the hunting and gathering groups of the Mesolithic era, whose stone tools and hunting weapons have been found on coastal and river-bank sites in North Wales. Agriculture, appearing in Britain about 5000 BC, marked the beginning of the New Stone Age or Neolithic period, and the following era between 4000 and 3000 BC is the first to leave visible and permanent evidence on the landscape of Snowdonia – the stone burial chambers.

The questions posed by these megaliths are still matter for speculation and may never be answered. It seems likely that some form of religion prompted the considerable efforts required to erect them, and that their purpose was to provide a place of communal burial over a long period. They were built from the fourth to the third millenium BC, the earlier types being usually portal dolmens (with a tilted capstone) covered with a long cairn of stones, and the later ones – passage graves – having an entrance leading to inner chambers where the remains of several persons were deposited. Round cairns covered these later tombs. More than sixty portal dolmens and passage graves are known in Gwynedd, a substantial number of them within the boundary of the national park. The most accessible site for the visitor is the one at Dyffryn Ardudwy (SH 588229), on the A496 coast road between Harlech and Barmouth, where the land on which the tombs stand once formed part of the playground of the village school. The larger of the two megalithic chambers is covered by a capstone ten feet square and two feet thick, which must have required considerable engineering skill to lift into place. The stones that lie scattered all round the two

Dyffryn Ardudwy tombs probably represent only a portion of the great cairn that once covered them. In the 5,000 years that have passed since it was built the cairn has no doubt supplied building material for houses and stone walls. Sometimes a megalithic tomb itself was used by later hill farmers as part of a wall, as can be seen in at least two places not far from Dyffryn Ardudwy – at Bron-y-foel Isaf on the seaward slopes of Moelfre and at Gwern Einion one and a quarter miles east of Llandanwg on the coast. The two cairns known as Carneddau Hengwm on the flanks of the Ardudwy hills (SH 613206), narrow parallel heaps of loose stones one of which is 150 feet long, were despoiled to build local walls and must once have been of great size. Despite its spoliation this is one of the most evocative prehistoric sites in Wales, and can be reached by walkers using a right of way that leaves the A496 a mile south of Tal-y-bont.

Quite different in atmosphere is the Capel Garmon Burial Chamber, an Ancient Monument near the village of Capel Garmon two and a half miles by road from Betws-y-Coed (SH 818543). Here a neatly fenced enclosure reached by a short footpath surrounds a well-preserved megalithic

Megalithic tombs at Dyffryn Ardudwy. The mass of stones spread round them formed a great cairn under which they were buried 5,000 years ago.

tomb with three chambers into which you can penetrate. Preservation is of course necessary if our heritage of prehistoric monuments is to remain, and remain accessible, to ourselves and our children; but it is the remote half-forgotten megalith high on the windy hillside that – for me at any rate – best evokes the primitive folk of that far-off time. And if the farmer at some later date has used the old stone tomb as part of his wall, that is symbolic of the continuity of life in Snowdonia.

Stone circles belong to a later period, from 3250 to 1800 BC. Their purpose is still an unsolved mystery, but it has been suggested that the uniformity in the layout of some circles indicates an early attempt at making an astronomical clock. One such circle is to be seen at Cefn Coch just over a mile south of Penmaenmawr, accessible by a steep public footpath. This path, incidentally, passes close to Graiglwyd, an important site, noted as a Neolithic 'factory' whence stone axe-heads are known to have been exported to places as distant as Stonehenge in Wiltshire (SH 720757).

The knowledge of metals and metal-working, established in the Orient from about 6000 BC, spread slowly across Europe and was brought as a

Visitors in the chambered tomb at Capel Garmon.

craft to Britain about 2000 BC, and about this time the first British bronzes were moulded. Bronze Age hoards – weapons, implements and ornaments – have been discovered at Bangor, Dolbenmaen, and many other places within the national park, and it is clear that for the next ten centuries the crafts of metal-working were slowly spreading in the inhabited parts of the region, chiefly round the coasts. Distribution of products involved the habitual use of routes which became, in time, well-beaten tracks and were even, in difficult places, roughly paved. The remains of these primitive trade routes are to be seen in many places throughout Snowdonia National Park. In the past they were often attributed mistakenly to the Romans, but finds of Bronze Age implements here and there along them indicate that they were in use many centuries before the Roman occupation. The trackway that crosses the Rhinog mountains at Bwlch Tyddiad above Cwmbychan, for instance, has long been famous as the 'Roman Steps', but it is now suggested that it was in use hundreds of years before the advent of the Romans, was perhaps improved and consolidated by them, and was further improved for the passage of pack animals in medieval times.

An ancient paved trackway near Croesor, locally called 'the Roman Road'. This track, like many others in Snowdonia, has probably been in use since prehistoric times.

One of the finest walks in the national park, full of archaeological interest, can be enjoyed by following the ancient trackway that starts from a lane crossroads a mile south east of Harlech and skirts the lower crags of the Rhinog mountains for the better part of twelve miles, finally disappearing into the waters of Llyn Trawsfynydd which closed above it when the lake became a reservoir. If you walk it (it is a right of way throughout) you'll find all along the route the traces of settlements and hut circles that show that these deserted hillsides were once inhabited; defended, too, for the trackway curves round the slopes of Moel Goedog (SH 613325), whose summit hillfort was a strong defensive position twenty-five centuries ago.

On this same trackway you'll pass several tall erect rocks, one of them eight feet high. Standing stones, called in Welsh *maen hir* (long stone), are yet another prehistoric mystery. They are often to be found beside the old tracks, and one of the best known, Llech Idris, stands close to the route followed by the Roman road or trackway known as Sarn Helen (SH 731311). This stone, eleven feet high, is situated in the upper valley of the River Gain where a falling glen leads southward towards

Llech Idris, eleven feet high, stands solitary in a hillside field near Trawsfynydd. Why this monolith was erected is not known, but it may have marked an old route running south into the Mawddach Valley.

Cadair Idris. An old story tells how the giant Idris threw this rock from the summit of the mountain ten miles away, and so provides its name. It can be reached by taking the motorable lane that climbs eastward from Bronaber, three miles south of Trawsfynydd on the A470; the stone stands in an enclosed field a few minutes' walk along a right of way track above the lane, and the farmer has provided access by marking with a white post the place where you can step across his fence.

A few hundred yards away from Llech Idris, on the other side of the motorable lane, is a rectangle of iron railings enclosing another antiquity, probably of much later date. This is Bedd Porius, the Grave of Porius, where an inscribed stone – nearly illegible now – bears the Latin words *Hic in tumulo iacit Porius. Homo planus fuit*. (Here in the mound lies Porius. An honest man was he.) Early speculation regarded this as the grave of a Roman centurion, but later authorities declare the stone to be a medieval monument. The present stone is a replica, the original having been removed in 1932 to the National Museum of Wales at Cardiff.

In the last millenium BC a folk migration which was to be perhaps the most significant event in

Welsh history was beginning its long slow movement from Central Europe. A group of heterogeneous peoples, later known in the classical world as the Celts, had evolved, in the Hallstatt area of Austria, an individual culture; they used iron as well as bronze, and in their later (La Tène) phase developed an artistic form and design in their products that rivalled the work of Greece and Rome. They were warriors as well as craftsmen, preserving the warlike deeds of their heroes as legends that were handed down by word-of-mouth from generation to generation. Celtic tribes speaking versions of the same tongue were on the move throughout Europe, northward and westward, and in course of time reached Britain and eventually spread into Wales, where the bearers of a Celtic culture may have formed a social élite in some areas. They were an aggressive and masterful folk who succeeded in establishing their own language wherever they settled. In England and Scotland this language was at length to be submerged beneath the successive impacts of other invading groups; but in Wales, isolated from those impacts by her barrier of mountains, it endured to become the basis of Primitive Welsh and evolve into the modern Welsh language.

Pen-y-gaer from Maen-y-bardd

The hillfort, of which there are many examples in Snowdonia, is one of the most distinctive monuments of the late first millenium in Britain, when Bronze Age man began his fort building. This period is equated with the colonizing activities of the Celts. The Ordnance Survey map shows the wide distribution of the hillforts; *caer*, *castell*, and *dinas* are all Welsh names signifying an ancient fortified position, and where you see them on the map there, probably, will be the remains of a hillfort. Mutation may cause the names to change to *ddinas* or *gaer*, as in Pen-y-gaer above the Conwy Valley in the north-east corner of the national park, where a hilltop nearly 1,300 feet above the sea was fortified by the men of the Iron Age (SH 750693).

Pen-y-gaer can be reached quite easily by way of the hillside village of Llanbedr-y-cennin which stands above the west bank of the river six miles south of Conwy; but for those who can walk three miles I recommend an approach from the village of Roewen, north of Llanbedr. An old track, the Roman route over Bwlch-y-ddeufaen to their fortress at Segontium, takes you past the megalithic tomb known as Maen-y-bardd, whence you see Pen-y-gaer ahead standing up finely against the sky, and making straight for it by footpath and lane you climb the hill as attacking warriors must often have done long ago. The nature of the defences is still plain to see. The outer and inner ramparts can be traced, enclosing an area 800 feet long by 500 feet wide in which the foundations of dwellings are visible. Outside a third rampart, which is now not continuous, two areas of *chevaux-de-frise* are laid, pointed rocks set in the ground to make things more difficult for the attackers who would probably be barefooted or shod with animal hide. The *chevaux-de-frise* defence is rare among the hillforts of England and Wales. So, one must add, is the view, on one side an eagle's-eye prospect over many miles of the Conwy Valley and on the other a stirring glimpse of the wild cwms under the summits of the Carneddau that heave themselves darkly against the western sky.

Another of the many hillforts deserves mention although it is a few miles outside the boundary of the national park. Tre'r Ceiri, which has been called 'the most remarkable Iron Age fort to be seen on this side of the Irish Sea', occupies the most easterly summit of the triple-peaked Yr Eifl, on the Lleyn Peninsula north of Pwllheli. Its name was given by the Welsh of a later date and means 'Town of

Giants', and is well suited to its extent and
massiveness. The huge ramparts and strategic
entrances are still there, and the remains of more
than a hundred stone dwellings in the big enclosed
area show that this was no emergency refuge but a
large permanent settlement with elaborate
defences. There is evidence that it was occupied for
a considerable time after the coming of the Romans.
To reach Tre'r Ceiri you make for the village of
Llithfaen on the B4417 road about seven miles north
of Pwllheli; from here a rough footpath (public right
of way) leads steeply up to the fort.

It has been suggested that settlements like Tre'r
Ceiri were tolerated or even encouraged by the
Roman invaders, who arrived in Snowdonia about
AD 70. They were concerned to control the country,
not to impose the Roman culture and way of life
upon it, so that some at least of the Celtic inhabitants
continued to live as they had done before while
others nearer the centres of Roman influence
gradually absorbed the ideas and methods of Rome.
Thus, unlike the rest of Britain, North Wales never
became truly Romanized. The purpose of the
legions was a holding-down one, repressing
opposition while the mineral wealth of Snowdonia
was exploited. It was garrisoned as a country under
military occupation, and such building as they did
was mainly for military purposes. When the legions
were withdrawn from Snowdonia to meet the
barbarian threat to Rome they left behind them,
besides the seeds of the Christian religion, a
number of forts or legionary bases. Perhaps the best
known and best preserved of these is Segontium
(SH 485625).

The National Trust has charge of the excavated
remains of Segontium and its Museum and they are
open to the public. They are outside the boundary
of the national park, on the right as you enter
Caernarfon by the A4085 road that runs from
Beddgelert through Rhyd-Ddu and Betws Garmon.
Here you can see the layout of what was for over 300
years the most important Roman post in Gwynedd,
established to control the warlike natives of north-
west Wales: the barrack blocks, centurions'
quarters, bath-houses, and regimental shrine. At
first probably a timber fort with a garrison of 1,000
men, Segontium was rebuilt in stone between AD 78
and the late fourth century, with a tower and a
guardhouse. From it the Romans made roads –
cleared tracks rather than the great highways they
made in England – to link Segontium with a small

At Caerhun in the Conwy Valley this fourteenth-century church occupies part of the site of the second-century Roman fort of Canovium.

fort twenty-five miles to the south and with their larger legionary base at Deva (Chester). This latter route crossed the foothills of the Carneddau mountains into the Conwy Valley by the pass of Bwlch-y-ddeufaen, and at the eastern foot of the pass they built a small fortified post which they called Canovium (SH 776703). All that is to be seen of the Canovium fortress now is an embanked square rising about five feet above field level close to the hamlet of Caerhun, on the A5106 south of Conwy. Excavations carried out here in the late 1920s established that a garrison of about 500 men occupied Canovium until the middle of the second century, when it became a civilian settlement. The fourteenth-century parish church of St Mary was built on the north-east quarter of the fort area.

The route of the southward Roman road from Segontium remains doubtful; but to reach the legionary base at the place now called Tomen-y-mur it must, in its southern part, have coincided with the old trackway known as Sarn Helen. Tomen-y-mur is a site conducive to reflection (SH 706387). It stands, symbol of the vanished power of Rome, confronting at a mile's distance a modern symbol of power, the atomic power station on the north shore of Trawsfynydd lake. Its Welsh name signifies a mound and a wall, and the mound (*tomen*) is in fact a castle motte built within the old fort enclosure by a Norman raiding-party in the time of William Rufus. A narrow lane mounting east from the A470 three miles south of Ffestiniog leads to a spot whence the *tomen* can be plainly seen, but the mound itself is on enclosed farm land for which permission to enter would be needed from the farmer. The motorable lane ends close beside a related site, marked on the map 'Roman Amphitheatre'. I've been told of some Italian visitors who went up there expecting to find something resembling the Colosseum and were disappointed; the amphitheatre is now just a circular depression between broken grass banks some twenty yards across, barely big enough (one would think) for two gladiators to manoeuvre in. Possibly it was designed for practice or instruction in the use of arms. The fact that it *was* constructed, and that traces of a parade-ground, bridge abutment and civil settlement have been discovered suggests that this remote legionary base was manned fairly continuously.

Tomen-y-mur, built in AD 79, stands beside the longest of the roads or routes built by the Romans in Wales: Sarn Helen. A romantic story in the Mabinogion tells how a Welsh princess, Elen, became the wife of the Roman deputy emperor Magnus Maximus and persuaded her husband to construct this road running from North Wales into South Wales, so that ever afterwards it bore her name. However, some archaeologists consider the name to be a corruption of *sarn y lleng*, meaning the causeway of the legion. Sarn Helen was not a permanent construction like the Watling Street or the Fosse Way, and there is very little to be seen nowadays in the way of paving or lateral ditches. In laying it out the Romans' purpose, probably, was to establish a route by which their legions could be moved from one trouble-point to another quickly and without encountering obstacles like bogs and precipices. Yet long stretches of it are continuous and can be followed by walkers, though in places it merges with the modern highways. If you were to follow Sarn Helen northward from Tomen-y-mur you would come in about three miles to a place where the Roman trackway, grassy but quite plain to see, enters the wild hills east of Ffestiniog. And here you would find a site which very well epitomizes the end of prehistoric times in Snowdonia.

Bryn-y-Castell is a small hilltop enclosure of the Iron Age standing above the little Afon Gamallt where it emerges from the mountains (SH 727429). You can get to it by taking the old hill road running eastward from Ffestiniog village for one and a half miles and then walking up a broad track northward for another half-mile; the site is marked 'Settlement' on the map. This is the first such site in the national park to be excavated completely, and the

The Roman trackway, Sarn Helen, comes down from the pass at top centre of this picture. The walker (bottom right) is following the way taken by the legionaries in the first century AD.

discoveries made have thrown additional light on the prehistoric way of life in Snowdonia. The finds included seamless glass bangles, scratched slate gaming-boards with black and white stones for pieces, and quantities of the fire-cracked rounded beach pebbles ('pot-boilers') which were heated in a fire and then used for cooking food or boiling water. Traces of two stake-wall roundhouses, the first to be found in Snowdonia, were discovered; these had consisted of a circular wall of stakes driven into the ground and bound with wattle and daub, and a roof of branches with perhaps a heather thatch. None of these materials would survive the centuries and only excavation can reveal the evidence of the stake-sockets, so there is no saying how many huts of this kind may have stood here and there in other corners of North Wales. Since estimates of the prehistoric population have hitherto been based on the visible stone circles of huts and concentrations of pottery fragments, it may be that the Iron Age folk were much more numerous than has been thought.

It was a succession of student teams from the Snowdonia National Park Study Centre at Plas Tan-y-Bwlch, directed by Peter Crew, who conducted these excavations from 1979 onwards. Perhaps their

most interesting discovery was that Bryn-y-Castell was a prehistoric iron-works. Over a ton of iron-working slag was recovered, equivalent to perhaps half a ton of finished iron, which is far more than such a settlement could have needed for its own use. This suggests very strongly that the iron was traded, locally and perhaps farther afield. It was smelted in small furnaces using local bog iron ore and charcoal fuel; at that time – a few years BC – the neighbouring hillsides that are today almost bare of trees would be largely covered in forest, so there would be no lack of wood for making the charcoal. Stone anvils and hammerstones, evidence that smithing was also done here, were found. When excavation was complete the site was reconstructed to show the line of the original defensive wall that rimmed the flat top of the hill, with its gateways and the position of the internal structures.

While it's unlikely that the builders of Bryn-y-Castell chose their site because of its view, that view is a splendid one, commanding the length of the

An imaginative reconstruction of an Iron Age stake-wall roundhouse.

Vale of Ffestiniog right to the sea. It makes a good starting point for a walk of eight miles or so which would trace Sarn Helen across those tangled hills to northward and down to Dolwyddelan in the Lledr Valley. But it also, in another way, makes a good finishing-point. The Iron Age folk in their little settlement typify the end of prehistory in Snowdonia. Down from the north, driving their road between the crags and through the forests, came the Roman builders of Sarn Helen, forerunners of a new era; and about AD 70 life at Bryn-y-Castell came to an end.

3 People and the environment

It has been said that developing peoples pass through two stages: first, the moulding and shaping of people by the environment; second, the moulding and shaping of the environment by people. This can be admitted if it is remembered that the processes are continuous, and that the environment of man's creation exerts as strong an influence upon him as did the natural environment of his prehistory. For the people who lived in what is now Snowdonia National Park, however, nature had provided an environment that was to influence their development for twenty centuries. They had a sea coast to west and north, but southward and particularly eastward stretched a wide barrier of mountains furrowed by valleys choked with dense forest. It was this barrier that cut off the inhabitants of northern Wales from the main tide of historical events in England, so that they preserved their developing nationality.

Into the Middle Ages and beyond it was proverbial that a man on a white horse might thread the forested valleys from south to north of Snowdonia without being seen, so thick and continuous were the woods. As to the mountains, they were trackless, haunted, impassable. East of the barrier, in England, Danes and Saxons invaded and settled and established their kingdoms, but very few of them succeeded in penetrating the mountain frontier. Within the barrier the Dark Ages show a tangled history of inter-tribal warfare, a coalescence of territories under emergent Welsh princes who later on were to establish uneasy contact with the Norman rulers of England.

Five centuries of contention between rival overlords, singly or in shifting alliance, saw the gradual emergence of three major 'kingdoms' – Gwynedd in the north west, Powys in the north east, Deheubarth in the south west – of which Gwynedd, towards the end of the period, became the most powerful. The prince of Gwynedd at the beginning of the thirteenth century was Llywelyn ap Iorwerth, who perhaps came nearer than any other man to his aim of uniting Wales under one ruler. A farsighted man and a skilful general, he deserves the title of Llywelyn the Great which posterity has awarded him. When Edward I began his determined conquest of Wales in the closing decades of the century he found in Gwynedd the hard core of Welsh resistance, and built his ring of castles to seal off Anglesey and Snowdonia from the rest of Wales.

Before and during these 500 years of struggle the Christian Church was slowly but surely establishing itself in Wales. It is accepted by most historians that the seeds of Christianity were sown in Britain by the Romans – after the conversion of the Emperor Constantine in AD 312 – and by travelling merchants. Wandering monks and holy men, the Celtic 'saints', spread the doctrine through Wales; monasteries were founded like that at St David's (mid-sixth century) and the priory of St Mary at Beddgelert (late sixth century) and hermits established their cells and holy wells. The cathedral of Bangor in Gwynedd was dedicated to St Deiniol in the sixth century, though no traces of this original foundation are now visible. Cymmer Abbey, the Cistercian monastery a mile north of Dolgellau, received its charter from Llywelyn ap Iorwerth in 1219. The bishoprics and monastic orders were

The Moelwyn range rises beyond the hidden Vale of Ffestiniog, standing between the huge slate mines of Blaenau Ffestiniog and the sea.

brought by Edward I under English control, and –
like the English Church – were administered from
Rome. Thenceforward the Christian Church in
Wales followed broadly the same historical path as
the Church in England.

Until the thirteenth century, when Edward
resolved to bring Wales into subjection to his rule,
the landscape of Snowdonia and the environment of
its inhabitants were not greatly changed from the
time of Roman occupation. Change began with the
building of the castles. There were castles – Welsh
castles – before Edward built his ring of great stone
fortresses. The warring princes had built
strongholds for themselves and so had the robber
chieftains who infested some parts of the country.
Castell Carndochan (SH 847307), two miles west of
Llanuchllyn on a crag above the Lliw Valley, is
probably one of the latter sort, and the ruined tower
on its lofty rock is highly evocative of these days
when Wales lay under:

> 'The good old rule, the simple plan
> That he should take who has the power,
> That he should keep who can.'

Castell Dolwyddelan with its square battlemented
keep (built in the thirteenth century to strengthen
older fortifications) is a Welsh castle in a better state
of preservation (SH 722523). Llywelyn the Great is
said to have been born in this lonely fortress,
constructed in the twelfth century to guard the long
Lledr Valley that cuts deep into the hills between
Snowdon and the Rhinog. Dolbadarn Castle, too,
was placed to command a valley, the narrow defile
leading to Llanberis Pass (SH 586598). Here is a
round keep of the thirteenth century within a
twelfth-century curtain wall, and today you can
stand where many an archer and spearman must
have stood and look from its ruined battlements up ·
the five-mile length of the craggy trough between
Snowdon and Glyder. Castell-y-Bere (SH 667086), in
the southern part of the national park two miles
north west of Abergynolwyn, was one of the largest
and most ornate of the Welsh castles, and in it
Llywelyn's brother Dafydd put up a stout defence
against King Edward's forces who had advanced up
the Dysynni Valley. The castle was taken and Dafydd
escaped into the fastnesses of Snowdon, perhaps
into the Carneddau whose second highest summit
bears his name. The castle today is a ruin,
destroyed by the victorious English in 1294; but you

The thirteenth-century keep of Castell Dolwyddelan has stood for 700 years overlooking the upper Lledr Valley.

can still see the remains of a rectangular keep, three towers, and a large triangular barbican. This is one of the pleasantest castle-sites to visit, not only for the interest of its extensive remains but also for the charm of its solitary position in the green valley beneath the southern bastions of Cadair Idris.

Edward I was not concerned to strengthen the Welsh inland strongholds for his own use, but castles on the sea coast fitted in nicely with his plan, which was to girdle Snowdonia with impregnable fortresses which, as he put it, must have 'their feet in the sea'. Supplied by ship, they had no need to depend upon the few and dangerous approach-routes by land. Criccieth Castle, built about 1200, was partly rebuilt and strengthened by Edward in 1282; suffered its greatest damage, ironically, at the hands of Owain Glyndŵr during his revolt against Henry IV; and today, with its venerable ruins perched above populous beaches and bright-sailed dinghies, adds to the charm of one of the prettiest seaside resorts in Wales. The first custodian of Criccieth Castle was a Welshman, Sir Hywel of the Axe, knighted by King Edward for his feat, at the battle of Poitiers, of cutting off the head of the French king's warhorse with one sweep of his famous pole-

axe. For 200 years after Hywel's death, says tradition, a dish of meat guarded by eight yeomen was set every day before his pole-axe in the castle courtyard and afterwards given to the poor.

Six miles distant across the waters of Tremadog Bay is Criccieth's sister castle, Harlech. This is surely the most romantically sited of all the castles of Snowdonia. High-perched, four-squared, round-towered and impressively massive, it dominates the coast north and south from its lofty rock and commands a splendid view of the Snowdonian summits beyond the wide Traeth Mawr where Glaslyn and Dwyryd flow together to reach the sea. Edward I built it at the end of the thirteenth-century; but it was its gallant defence in the Wars of the Roses by a Welsh supporter of the Red Rose, Dafydd ap Ifan ap Einion, with an outnumbered handful of soldiers, that inspired the famous 'Men of Harlech' song. Less than 300 years ago the castle surrendered, after a siege, to one of Oliver Cromwell's generals; it was the last of the Royalist strongholds to be taken. To look down from its vertiginous battlements with its seven centuries of history in mind is to glance, however fleetingly, into the violent world of the past.

Harlech Castle from the north, a view resembling the painting by JMW Turner of this famous fortress.

Today Harlech Castle does not have its 'feet in the sea', though (as its Water Gate shows) it did when it was built; the nearest waves, breaking on the grandest stretch of sandy beach in all Wales, are half a mile away beyond the encroaching dunes that have provided an equally fine golf-course. Caernarfon Castle and Conwy Castle still stand at the sea's edge, each in its own way different from

The dunes of Morfa Harlech, with the four mile long sandy beach beyond.

Harlech though both are Edwardian castles. The huge fortress at Caernarfon is the largest of them, an irregular oblong covering two and a half acres of ground with its massive walls and thirteen great towers, one of them – the Eagle Tower – 124 ft (38 m) high. Edward's son, the first English Prince of Wales, was born here, and the throne where subsequent Princes of Wales have sat at their investitures is one of the things to see. For my part, I prefer Conwy Castle to Caernarfon. Here, as at Caernarfon, Edward I planted a complete new town within a battlemented enclosure, making it a large additional ward of the castle; and at Conwy you get a good idea of what a thirteenth-century defended town was like because it has retained its circuit of medieval walls quite complete – one of the very few towns in the British Isles to have done so. The quay Edward built for his supply ships is still there, too. And I like the small garden on a castle terrace overlooking the river which was devised for Edward's queen, Eleanor of Castile; they say the first sweet peas ever seen in Britain were grown there, from seed brought from Eleanor's native land.

Like other historic monuments in the national

park, these castles are in the care of Cadw (meaning heritage), the Welsh organization originating from the Welsh Office with subsequent outside recruitment, which now maintains 127 ancient monuments in Wales.

The castle-building age did more than add a number of large buildings to the seaward landscape of Snowdonia. The presence of the fortresses effectively deterred the hordes of pirates, from Ireland and elsewhere, that for centuries had been making life difficult for dwellers on the fertile slopes above the coast. Ports and villages, agriculture and stock raising – all the developments that were to make a real change in the environment – were given a chance to accelerate the growth that had been going on all this long time. For while the kings and the great lords and their armies had been rampaging to and fro across Snowdonia, ordinary people had been busy extracting a living from their countryside. One continuing result of their activities was the gradual removal of the forests.

Trees – wood – had of course been used from the earliest times. They were needed for fuel and spear-shafts and ships, then for houses and furniture and fences and countless other things. Now, with the growth of population and the extension of farming, trees were felled to make room for crop-growing fields or pasturage for cattle. Besides the farmsteads pushing up into the valleys, there were shepherds pasturing large and growing flocks and herds on the higher ground; not many sheep at first, but a great many goats. Goats and sheep were to play an important part in the destruction of the forests.

In *A History of Gwynedd* (1983) it is estimated that at the time of the Norman conquest of England sixty per cent of Snowdonia was covered by forest; nine centuries later that has been reduced to only three per cent, and the goats had quite a lot to do with it. From the Dark Ages to the end of the seventeenth century they were probably the most numerous of the pasture animals in Wales, and to the English the goat was as much a symbol of Welshness as the leek. 'Not for Cadwallader and all his goats!' cries Pistol in *Henry V* when Fluellen tries to get him to eat a leek. Even when the more profitable mountain sheep began to exceed them in numbers, big herds were still maintained, and in 1774 Doctor Samuel Johnson, boating with Mrs Thrale's small daughter on Llanberis lake, was able to count 149 goats on the lakeside slopes; it was eighteenth-century fashion that brought them there, for goat's-hair was

Feral goats, descendants of the flocks kept by the Welsh chieftains and their followers before the era of the mountain sheep

Mixed woodland in Gwydyr Forest. Forestry policy today is to plant more indigenous deciduous trees among the conifers.

essential for the gentlemen's wigs. Their day was nearly over then but their work of destruction was carried on by the sheep. The rapidly multiplying flocks, marching and countermarching through the upper forests, ate every growing seedling, thus preventing the growth of trees to replace those that died or were felled.

So the forests slowly passed and slowly open pasture land took their place. At first cattle, rather than sheep, grazed these pastures. Beef cattle grazed up to the highest ground, and the hardy 'runts', forerunners of the world-famous Welsh Blacks, could thrive where milking cows could not. Cattle became a valuable export, supplying the growing demand in England, and the trade that grew from this had a marked effect on the lives of the people of Snowdonia. It also left its mark on the landscape: a network of drove roads.

From the late Middle Ages to well into the nineteenth century the drovers made their epic annual journeys, right across Wales and England to the markets in the east Midlands, East Anglia, and Barnet and Smithfield in the London area. It took them two months to get there with their droves of up to 400 cattle attended by half a dozen drovers and their dogs. Roads being bad or non-existent, they made their own regular routes, keeping when possible to the open high ground where it was easier to control their charges. The big herds from the lowland pastures of Lleyn and Anglesey, having swum the Menai Strait at low water, would join the Snowdonian herds or take their own northern route if they were not bound for the south; in 1810 it was recorded that 14,000 'Welsh Runts' were arriving in

'Welsh Blacks', grazing near Dolgellau.

the Midlands annually from Lleyn and Anglesey alone. The London markets had been a favourite destination for the droves from Snowdonia for a long time, and the worth of their contribution to the English economy may be judged from a letter written to Prince Rupert about 1645 wherein the writer describes the cattle-droves as 'the Spanish Fleet of North Wales, which brings hither that little gold and silver we have'. Often the droves included geese and pigs, and these like the cattle were specially shod for the long journey. The hooves of the cattle were protected with quarter-circle metal shoes called 'cues', the pigs were given little woollen socks with leather soles such as children wore, and the geese – for whom the two-month journey must have been a great ordeal – were driven, before starting, through a mixture of tar and sand which would harden into a protective covering. The noise made by this heterogeneous cavalcade on the march must have been deafening, the voices of 400 cattle mingling with those of geese and pigs and augmented by the barking of the dogs and the drovers' shouts of 'Heiptro Ho!'

Many of the drovers' roads in the national park are today metalled hill roads, like the delightful unfenced road (labelled now B4391) that crosses the moorland hills from Ffestiniog to Ysbyty Ifan. Others can be seen still as broad grass tracks. One of the most interesting to walk on foot can be picked up at Cors-y-gedol a mile east of Dyffryn Ardudwy and followed over the 1,500-foot pass of Bwlch-y-Rhiwgyr (SH 627201), passing the old cottage of Llety Loegr which was once a shoeing-station and overnight shelter for drovers, down to the

The Welsh Mountain breed of sheep is one of the handsomest of its kind, and its lambs have a toy-like charm.

Mawddach Valley. The special interest of this route is that towards the end of the coaching era it was roughly paved and became – unlikely as it must seem to anyone walking it today – part of the London to Harlech coach road.

The drovers played an important part in the breaching of the barrier between the people of Snowdonia and the country from which they were now being governed. With the returning drovers came all the news from London and the English markets; news of the latest agricultural techniques and developments in stock-breeding. Their roads brought isolated villages and farms into closer contact and sometimes (as with the London to Harlech road) initiated long-distance communication. But the cattle boom dwindled as wool increased in economic importance, and new markets brought into prominence an animal already pasturing extensively on the hills of Snowdonia: the Welsh Mountain sheep.

If the goats made their impact on the landscape with the reduction of the forests, the sheep made theirs with the proliferation of stone walls, many of them now two centuries old. Except on the mountain tops (and sometimes even there) you see stone walls, wherever you look in the national park. Enclosing valley fields, sweeping arrow-straight up a mile of mountainside, curled in mysterious patterns in some remote cwm, they lay their grey lines and scrolls on the green and gold and purple of foreground and distance. They were built to make the hard work of the sheep farmer easier, and because the Welsh Mountain is a particularly active breed and a good leaper they were built strong and high. If you accidentally knock a few rocks off the top of such a wall you have probably given the farmer an extra day's work recovering the sheep that will escape.

Some of these walls are miracles of ingenuity and craftsmanship. One that never fails to excite my admiration is the wall that runs for six miles from the summit of Y Llethr in the Rhinog (SH 661258), 2,457 ft (749 m) above the sea, right along the crest of the Llawlech ridges to end above Barmouth. It is a beautifully built drystone wall, its rocks fitted so neatly that you would think the builders had unlimited material to choose from; yet the broad grassy crests over which it dips and rises, Crib-y-rhiw and Diffwys, are now completely devoid of suitable rocks. Another crest-wall crosses Moel Hebog, above Beddgelert, not defending a precipice-verge like the one on Y Llethr but marking a boundary between hill farms. On the slopes lower down you'll come to the mountain-wall, an important barrier sealing off the *mynydd*, the high mountain sheep-run, from the *ffridd* or lower pastures into which the sheep will be brought in winter. Below again are the enclosed fields near the farmhouse.

Like many others to be seen, the old stone walls in this picture have been allowed to fall into ruin, the purpose for which they were built having ceased to exist. They remain, often in astonishing situations, as evidence of patient work in a skilled craft.

On a stormy day, when Moel Hebog wears a crown of angry cloud, Llyn Gwynant still retains its wild beauty.

In the national park today the tendency is for hill farms to be grouped into larger units. The higher farmhouses become derelict or are leased as holiday homes, and the pastures are taken over by a bigger farming concern in the valley whose shepherds will probably climb to the higher ground by tractor, Land Rover, or motor-cycle when gathering is necessary. Fifty years ago the small hill farm could still thrive, and in some areas (in the Ffestiniog hills, for example) the old pattern of life survives, unchanged for centuries. Here two or three farms work together when the seasonal needs arise. The gathering, which precedes the shearing and dipping, is done on each of the farms in turn, the men from the other farms joining in to help. This is the big event of the year for the farmer's wife, too. She has to provide of her best for the small army of hungry helpers; not forgetting their dogs, who usually regard these once-yearly encounters as heaven-sent opportunities for combat. The shearing is done with the same neighbourly help, generally with electric clippers though a few farmers still use the formidable hand-shears that were used by their great-grandfathers. The branding (with dye of various colours) is done while the sheep's feet are

Hill farms like this one at the head of Llyn Cwmbychan often have few amenities beyond beauty of situation. Today their high-mountain pastures tend to be farmed from more comfortable dwellings nearer to shops and roads.

still tied for the shearing. Co-operation between adjacent farms is part of the pattern. The maze-like groups of stone-walled folds you will see beside a mountain stream in some upland cwm are built that way to an age-old plan and with specific purposes in mind. The stream, you'll find, has been dammed to make a deep pool for sheep-washing, and often this was used by two hill farms, as indicated by the sketch-plan which shows one such arrangement.

Nowadays there's no such thing as mutton; it's all Welsh lamb. The flesh of the Welsh mountain sheep was renowned for its tastiness at least as early as the fourteenth century, and at that period also its wool and the products that were made from it were very

A plan of sheepfolds used by two farms. A— reception pens; B—pens for ewe lambs; C— sorting pen; D— strangers' pen (stray sheep); E—washing pen; BW—farm boundary wall; G—gaps closed by small grills.

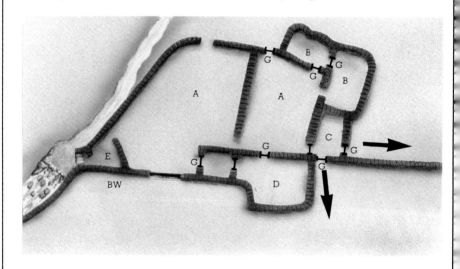

The woollen mill at Trefriw is one of several in Snowdonia that still maintain the crafts that were important to the economy two centuries ago.

important to the economy of Snowdonia. The spinning-wheel was part of the furniture in most cottages, the weaving of woollen cloth was widespread in the small towns and villages, and woollen articles were exported from the one or two small ports on the Ardudwy coast. Bala was the centre of this wool trade. Today it is chiefly famous as having on its doorstep the largest natural lake in the national park, Llyn Tegid, and the best 'inland' dinghy sailing in Wales; while close at hand is the Afon Tryweryn, a canoeist's river and scene of the 1981 World Championships. But you can still see, a little way off Bala High Street, the ancient *tomen* or mound (once a castle motte) where long ago the inhabitants of Bala – men and children as well as women – used to sit on fine evenings knitting away at socks and stockings. And not so very long ago, either. In 1805, it is recorded, from two to five hundred pounds worth of stockings were being sold from here every week. In those days that was a very considerable sum; and if the record is to be believed it implies that everyone in Bala worked remarkably hard and at remarkable speed.

The woollen trade still thrives in the national park, though in a rather different environment, and so does its essential basis the sheep. You can follow the whole process from lamb to rug by visiting some of its present-day sites. There are farm trails like the one at Cefn-Isa, two miles east of Llanbedr, that tell the story of Welsh hill farming, and there are working woollen mills – at Dinas Mawddwy, Penmachno, Bryncir, Trefriw and elsewhere – where you can see all the processes by which the sheep's woolly coat becomes a pair of socks or a smart costume. You won't, however, see the train of sturdy ponies which in earlier times carried these products overland to the coast for seaborne distribution.

The pack trains from Bala, for instance, had a journey of thirty miles to make before they reached the sea at Harlech or Llanbedr, and though parts of the old trackway are sunk in morasses or lost through disuse it can be followed through the upper glens of Lliw and Gain and seen famously where it crosses Bwlch Tyddiad by way of the 'Roman Steps' (SH 657300). This deservedly well-known pass was possibly in use before the time of the Romans and probably used by them, but the Steps themselves, those five hundred or so stone slabs paving one of the wildest defiles in the national park, were almost certainly emplaced in medieval times to take the

increased traffic between Bala and the coast. From their western foot the old track descends to Llyn Cwmbychan and along its northern shore (a motorable lane runs there now) to follow the Artro River down its glen to Llanbedr. The mile-long stretch of the A496 that runs northward from the village to Pensarn is still called – and so named on the map – 'Sarn Hir', the Long Causeway; it ends at the old quay just below the Llanbedr and Pensarn halt of the British Rail Cambrian Coast line, and here a small coasting brig would take on board the ponies' loads and bear them away to market. They might go south to Barmouth and Aberystwyth or even northward round Bardsey to the small but growing port of Liverpool. And the ship would be one of many that were plying in and about Cardigan Bay, for seafaring had been an integral part of the economy of Gwynedd for hundreds of years.

Today's visitor to Snowdonia National Park finds its coastal waters and little ports used almost exclusively by pleasure craft, but the men of Gwynedd have a very long tradition of seamanship behind them. From the twelfth century when Madoc, prince of Gwynedd, is said to have twice crossed the Atlantic (incidentally discovering America three centuries before Columbus) to the outbreak of the First World War there was not only a busy seaborne trade but also a shipbuilding industry. The ships were for the most part small sloops and brigs. Often they were built on open beaches as well as in the ports from the Mawddach to the Conwy estuaries, and some were for the thriving herring fisheries of Barmouth and Aberdyfi. Herrings have declined in these waters since the seventeenth century, and if you go fishing off the estuaries of Dyfi and Mawddach and Glaslyn nowadays you are more likely to be trolling for mackerel than netting for herring.

The heyday of shipbuilding and seafaring on the coasts of Snowdonia came in the mid-nineteenth century. Between 1830 and 1890, it is recorded, as many as 300 ships were built at Pwllheli with a total tonnage of 13,415, while at the much younger port of Porthmadog 446 ships were built totalling nearly 30,000 tons. The cause of this shipbuilding boom was the rapid development of the slate industry.

Slate was to leave a heavy mark on the landscape of Snowdonia. To the people of many mountain villages its mining or quarrying brought a drastic change of environment, as can be seen today. Driving through Blaenau Ffestiniog or Corris, or

Bwlch Tyddiad crosses the Rhinog range east of Llanbedr, and the paved way that takes it through one of the wildest defiles in Wales has long been known as the Roman Steps. The Romans may well have used the pass, but the Steps are now thought to have been emplaced in medieval times.

In Cwmorthin, above Tan-y-grisiau, the 'mountains' of slate spoil confront the higher and older mountains of the Moelwyn range.

walking up the Cwmorthin Valley, you enter a world where the mountains are man-made, enormous hills of slate spoil. When you look up from the Llanberis lakes and see the whole huge flank of Elidir Fawr carved into dark artificial precipices it seems that a giant has been at work; and indeed it took thousands of men a hundred years of hard and sometimes dangerous labour to produce these ineradicable scars.

The national park boundary skirts round the main slate-quarrying centres – Llanberis, Bethesda, Nantlle, Blaenau Ffestiniog and Corris – but there are many smaller quarries within the park, some of them impressive open-cast workings hidden away among wild hills, left just as they were when the quarrymen abandoned them. I have a particular fondness for the old Drum quarry in the Ffestiniog hills (SH 430735). (There is no public footpath to it and it would perhaps be wise to obtain permission.) Drum quarry is quite close to Bryn-y-Castell, the Iron Age enclosure mentioned in the previous chapter. You can reach it in twenty minutes or so by mounting the broad track that runs north west below Bryn-y-Castell, and it's worth climbing the zigzags past the quarry faces to look at the lonely little Llyn-y-Drum in its rocky hollow above. Looking across the level quarry bottoms to the bare slaty crags that tower above them, you get a good idea of the conditions in which the quarrymen worked the open-cast sites, dangling precariously on the rock-face, perhaps in driving rain, plying their iron 'jumper' rods to bore holes for the blasting charges.

The slate mines at Blaenau Ffestiniog are far larger than this (one of the two open to visitors is

From roofing material to billiard tables, slate found a wide range of uses. Here slate slabs have been used to make a fence.

said to be the largest in the world) and these enormous caverns resulted from the following underground of a big vein of slate. The principal slate bed here is 120 ft (36.5 m) thick in places and dips downward into the mountainside at an angle of between twenty and thirty degrees. To get at such a bed, the first operation was to drive an adit through the rock alongside it so as to reach the upper surface of the slate. Then the first level would be taken out sideways above the surface, after which the series of parallel chambers across the slate bed could be begun, wide pillars or walls of rock being left as roof-supports between them. Inclined drifts or 'roofs' were carved out up the side of the proposed chamber and this sideways widening continued until the chamber was 40 or 50 ft (12 or 15 m) wide, and the roof further excavated at the same time so as to increase the air-space as quickly as possible. The atmosphere in the workings while this was going on was thick with slate dust and breathing was difficult; nearly all slate quarrymen suffered sooner or later from silicosis.

All the work so far was done by the 'miners', whose job was quite distinct from that of the 'rockmen' or slate-getters, who now began to rend away the blocks of slate with carefully calculated charges of blasting-powder and then to lever them clear for lowering and transporting out of the mine. Light narrow-gauge rails were laid for the small trucks that removed the waste rubble and the slate, which would be pushed by hand on the level stretches and lowered by a pulley system down the rails of the steep inclines. In the cutting-sheds below, the blocks were cut to a required size by

Slate tombstones throng the churchyard at Llandanwg near Harlech. Many of them bear fine examples of slate engraving.

machinery, usually operated by a wheel driven by water power, and then – if it was roofing slates that were wanted – the 'dressers' would take over, using the *cŷn manhollt* or broad chisel to split the blocks into thin slates by placing the blade parallel to the cleavage line and striking it with a wooden mallet. No machine was ever evolved to substitute for the human hand in this highly skilled job.

From the Ffestiniog quarries the slates were taken to the coast for export by sea. Before 1836 they were loaded into barges at quays on the Dwyryd estuary and taken out on the tide to waiting ships; at that time the sea at spring tides came in nearly to Aberglaslyn (*aber* = river-mouth) and you can still see there, a hundred yards below the bridge, one of the old quays. But in 1811 the enterprising W A Madocks built the mile-long embankment known nowadays as The Cob, preventing the sea from flooding the Glaslyn estuary, and as a by-product of his land-reclamation scheme a harbour was formed and the town of Porthmadog sprang up. The quarries seized this opportunity and constructed a narrow-gauge tramway nine miles long from Blaenau Ffestiniog to Porthmadog, with a continuous gradient so that the loaded trains could run down by gravity, the horses that would haul the empties up again travelling in special wagons at the rear of the train. By 1863 steam locomotives had taken the place of the horses, as they had on the Tal-y-llyn narrow-gauge line that connected Tywyn with the Nant Gwernol slate quarries south of Cadair Idris (SH 685065). And for Porthmadog this was the beginning of an Age of Sail that lasted nearly a century.

Brigs, barques, and barquentines, but especially the famous two-masted and three-masted schooners, carried Welsh slates all over the world. Slate shipments from Porthmadog soon reached a yearly tonnage of 65,000. Apart from the cargoes taken to home ports, slates were carried to Germany and the North European ports and not infrequently across the Atlantic to South America. These were all small vessels between 100 and 300 tons, and their captains and crews were almost without exception men from the coasts and villages of Snowdonia. By 1880 the cargo tonnage carried had doubled and no less than 469 different ships were using Porthmadog harbour regularly. But at the end of the century the slate industry was beginning its decline. 1937 found only fourteen quarries still working instead of the forty-seven of fifty years earlier. Rising production costs, foreign competition, and increasing use of roofing tiles were having their effect; and though for a while there was a continuing demand for the slate slabs used in making billiard tables, laboratory benches, and electrical switchboards, the industry's importance in Snowdonia was at an end.

As for the fleet of little ocean-going ships, that too had to pass, with the coming of railways that could transport the slates to Liverpool and the cargo steamers. The Maritime Museum at Porthmadog tells something of their story, and here alongside lies the *Garlandstone*, one of the few surviving barques, to give visitors who go on board an idea of what life at sea was like in the days of sail.

The products of the various metal-mining activities in Snowdonia added little if anything to the seaborne trade of those days. Before and since the Roman occupation of the country small mines have been worked, sporadically and intermittently, but only in a few instances has the ore proved rich enough for any large-scale enterprise. Copper and lead mines have left evidence of assiduous working in the eighteenth and nineteenth centuries, and a walk through the Gwydyr forest north of Betws-y-Coed over to Llyn Geirionydd takes you past some of the old lead mines. If you start from Gwydyr Castle you will pass a wide grassy meadow which was once a large and extremely ugly plain of lead-mine spoil; nothing will grow on lead spoil, but here it has been covered with turf and an eyesore removed. The Snowdon Copper Mines whose ruins stand beside the Miners' Track close to Llyn Llydaw prospered during the late nineteenth century, so

much so that the causeway across the end of Llydaw was constructed for the cartloads of ore. Before this a large raft, with the horse and loaded cart on it, used to be floated across the lake – until it capsized one day, luckily without loss of life. Above the A498 road where it leaves Beddgelert to head up Nant Gwynant you can see on the right the orange-red screes that are part of the spoil from the old Sygun Fawr copper mines (SH 605488), which were worked off and on from 1720 to about 1904 and are now open to visitors. The upper workings of these mines make an interesting item on one of the pleasantest low-level walks in this part of the park, which starts from the car park a quarter-mile east of Aberglaslyn bridge and goes up the pretty glen of Cwm Bychan to cross a miniature pass over to Llyn Dinas. In the upper part of the valley are the remains of the wire-cable system by which the buckets of copper ore were brought down to be loaded on the trucks of the Welsh Highland Railway; the railway used to come from Beddgelert through the tunnel under the Aberglaslyn ridge and crossed the embankment just above the car park on its way to Porthmadog.

Gold has been mined in several places in the

The hills now covered by the Gwydyr Forest were once a lead-mining area. This old lead mine stands above the lane leading to Llyn Geirionydd.

national park, notably in the area north of the Mawddach Valley, but as with the other metals there is insufficient to support large operations. Gold for royal wedding-rings has come from the Gwynfynydd mine (SH 734281) near Ganllwyd (where, currently, work has started again) and from the Clogau mine, sometimes called St David's, above Bontddu. But none of these undertakings made such a lasting impact on Snowdonia as the mining of slate. Not only the spoil-heaps of the mines, but also the villages and mansions built by the mine owners, changed and – sometimes – enhanced the landscape. Lord Penrhyn, for instance, built cottages and a church at Bethesda for his miners and a castle for himself; and the Oakeleys of Ffestiniog built the fine mansion of Plas Tan-y-Bwlch which is now the Snowdonia National Park Study Centre.

Throughout the era of mineral-getting activity, however, agriculture remained the basic industry in Gwynedd. The success of the drovers at the English markets had induced a change of balance in the farming pattern, and from the sixteenth to the early eighteenth century cattle, rather than sheep, dominated the scene. This involved the movement

Small villages with farms scattered among the surrounding meadows and hills are typical of northern Snowdonia outside the mountain region.

of the herds to summer pastures on the mountains. The herdsmen and their families moved in late spring to the upper dwelling, called the *hafod*, where they remained until the coming of autumn, returning then with the butter and cheeses made at the *hafod* to resume residence at the *hendre* (old, or permanent, house) through the winter. This custom of transhumance was ending by the beginning of the nineteenth century, when the successful introduction of root crops made winter fodder available. But the ruins of the old *hafodau* can be seen high on the hillsides still, and the custom is commemorated in farmhouse names like Hafotty (summer dwellings) or Plas Hendre.

The rise of the slate industry in Snowdonia had coincided closely with another development that was to influence the way of life of the people and add another distinctive feature to their environment. This was the Methodist revival. Originating in South Wales, this wave of religious enthusiasm spread to North Wales largely through the devotion of Thomas Charles (you'll see his statue in Tegid Street, Bala) who founded the British and Foreign Bible Society. Few ancient monuments in the national park are so moving as the little monument at Tyn-y-ddôl, half a mile north of Llanfihangel-y-pennant in the Dysynni Valley (SH 673096), which records how in the year 1800 Mary Jones, aged eighteen, walked the thirty-odd miles to Bala and back to obtain a Welsh Bible from Mr Charles; and Mary's action symbolizes the fervour with which the new religion – for such in effect it was – gripped the people not only of the country districts but of the new industrial regions as well. The great majority of the population of Snowdonia became Methodists, and the chapel became the centre of social life, dominating all activities.

'It is difficult,' writes David Williams in his *History of Wales*, 'to exaggerate the influence of the Methodist revival on the Welsh nation. It changed the tone of the whole people. The carefree life of the earlier period was displaced by a religious earnestness which put an end to many a harmless custom.' The enthusiasm was widespread, chapel membership became universal. The new villages that sprang up with the extension of the quarries were named from the Bible – Bethesda, Nazareth, Nebo – and the quarrymen were as thoroughly imbued with the religious spirit as the rest of the community. In the quarry barracks, where most of them lived for six days of the week, the evening

The monument to Mary Jones stands within the roofless walls of the old cottage that was her home.

The chapels of Snowdonia are not remarkable for beauty, but their numbers testify to the fervour of the religious revival in the nineteenth century.

discussions centred on the sermons they had heard in the village chapel on Sunday, and (to quote David Williams's *History* again) 'the passing of judgement on pulpit oratory became the favourite occupation of Welshmen everywhere and at all times'. It was the nightly hymn-singing at many quarries that originated the male-voice choirs that can be heard in Snowdonia today, some of them internationally famous. And this was the great age of chapel-building. Every village and town built its chapel, giving it a Biblical name like Salem or Bethel, and every Sunday it was packed to the doors. But this was not to last.

The small village of Croesor (SH 631448) on the seaward slope of the Moelwyn mountains exemplifies the changes that took place between about 1830 and 1930. Nowadays there is a small car park with a National Park information board at Croesor, for it is the starting place for the popular route to the top of Cnicht (2,265 ft, [690 m]) and the ridge-walk over the two Moelwyns. The chapel you see dominating the village was once twice its present size, having been enlarged to accommodate the growing congregations as the Rhosydd and Croesor quarries at the end of the valley expanded. In those days there was a butcher's shop and a tailor at Croesor and its few cottages must have been crowded to their utmost capacity. Now the chapel has been reduced again to its original size to save maintenance costs, and half the cottages are empty except in the summer when they are let as holiday accommodation.

The big congregations and their religious fervour have gone. But the chapels remain, as characteristic

a feature of Snowdonia as the stone walls on its
hillsides though in most cases a good deal less
pleasing to look at, with their ostentatious façades
that have been called 'the most outrageous mixtures
of Romanesque derivatives that cement can
produce'. Nevertheless, one or two of the big
chapels in the towns, such as Tabernacl at
Porthmadog, are worth a look inside, if only for their
vast size and spacious galleries and the fine
woodwork to be seen. Chapel attendance is by no
means dead – far from it; but today's religious
observances are on a much diminished scale and on
a broader and more tolerant basis.

A very strict observance of the Sabbath day came
with the Methodist revival. In part, perhaps, it was a
reaction from the eighteenth-century days of
decadent Anglicanism in North Wales, when – as
was the custom at the little church of Penmorfa –
cockfights were held in the churchyard after
Service. The men of the slate-carrying schooners,
no less than the slate-miners, upheld the stern tenet,
which persisted until quite recently. When I first
came to live on the coast of Snowdonia in 1946 the
seaside village was in effect ruled by the chapel,
whose deacons were nearly all retired sea-captains.
By them it was ordained that no craft of any kind
should put out on the waters of the bay on a Sunday.
The only exception to this rule was when, as
sometimes happened, a boat broke from its
moorings in stormy weather and was in danger of
drifting on the rocks; and then it was pleasant to see
the competition among the old seamen in their
Sunday blacks as to who should put out to the
rescue. Now, for better or worse, Sunday is hardly
different from any other day, and the bay is
crowded with bright sails and boats full of happy
children.

For the visitor to Snowdonia, the holiday-maker
wanting to enjoy every minute of his break from
work, this release from the rigour of Sabbatarianism
was welcome. And tourism had already begun its
rapid growth before the heyday of slate was over.

Snowdonia was not entirely unknown to the
English before tourism began to influence its people
and their environment. One or two bold spirits,
usually botanists, had made the difficult journey into
the mountains in the seventeenth century and
written about their exploits. One of them, Thomas
Johnson, climbed Snowdon as early as 1639 and
recorded his impressions: 'We reached at last the
highest ridge of the mountain, which was wrapped

Early travellers on the London to Holyhead road saw the barren mountains of the Nant Ffrancon as a wilderness to shudder at.

in cloud. Here the way is very narrow, and the climber is horror-stricken by the rough and rocky steeps on either hand and the Stygian marshes both on this side and that.' A hundred years later Joseph Cradock wrote of the Pass of Aberglaslyn that it was 'the last Approach to the mansion of Pluto through the regions of Despair'. Horror and classical allusion were the keynotes of most early accounts, but the advent of the Lake poets with their truer celebration of natural scenery changed this attitude, and in the next century George Borrow's *Wild Wales* gave his readers a fuller idea of the interest of Wales and its people. By Borrow's time Snowdon at least had become a popular objective with tourists, for when he climbed it with his step-daughter Henrietta from Llanberis they found 'groups of people, or single individuals, going up or descending the path as far as the eye could reach'. This was in 1854. Telford's great London to Holyhead road had been built by then, and numbers of coach travellers on the way to Ireland had seen the fine peaks that flank the Nant Ffrancon pass. But only the wealthy and leisured classes could afford the time and money for a holiday in North Wales, and most of these preferred to travel to the more fashionable Swiss Alps or Italian Lakes.

Even the comparatively small numbers of early visitors to Snowdonia were enough for the foundation of a new industry, however. Large and comfortable hotels were built to accommodate them in the coaching days of the first half of the nineteenth century; the Royal Goat at Beddgelert and the Royal Hotel (now Plas-y-Brenin, the National Centre for

The beach at Barmouth has plenty of sand for traditional castle-building and its craggy hinterland provides footpath walks with splendid sea views.

Mountain Activities) at Capel Curig are two of these. Local men set up as guides, or rangers as they called themselves. The original Snowdon ranger, John Morton, who first opened the Snowdon Ranger Inn (now a Youth Hostel) by the shore of Llyn Cwellyn (SH 565551), instituted his own guided route up Snowdon in opposition to the old Llanberis Path. Cadair Idris had its professional guides, too, and other men of the region, spreading a wider net, tempted the tourist with advertisements like this one displayed in 1819:

> Richd. Pugh, guide-general to the Tremendous mountain of Cadair Idris; the Astonishing watter-falls of Dolmelynllyn, Cin, and Mawddach: and the Most Wonderful Oak-tree at Llettyrhys, the Boughs of which measure One Hundred Yards in circumference.

But it was the coming of the railways that made tourism into a profitable industry for large numbers of the people of Snowdonia. It coincided with the minor social revolution that gave families in the crowded industrial North and Midlands of England better wages and longer holidays, and for these the

The Pyg track up Snowdon, so called because it crosses Bwlch-y-moch, the Pass of the Pigs. Heavy foot-traffic on this popular path has required consolidation work by national park wardens, as can be seen in this picture.

annual seaside holiday became an institution. The Great Western lines along the north coast and by way of Llangollen and Bala to Barmouth, and the Cambrian line opening up the west coast, changed ports and villages into seaside resorts, and instead of chapels and slate-miners' cottages the new building was of hotels and guest-houses and boarding accommodation. The satellite villages east and west of Llandudno blossomed into 'fronts' and promenades, and the Meirionnydd coast with its many sandy beaches became a thriving holiday area, especially at Barmouth and Aberdyfi, which soon established themselves firmly in tourist favour.

A growing number of younger and more active folk began to discover the beauties of inland Snowdonia on foot; among these the 'walking-tour' became a popular form of holiday early in the 1900s, and from 1906 to 1926 the Great Western Railway was engaged in a tourist promotion of North Wales as 'The British Tyrol', with excursion tickets and carriage pictures showing the mountains and valleys. Rock climbing brought its increasing numbers of devotees who built their club huts among the mountains or took over and converted derelict barns, Youth Hostels sprang up after 1930; a growing emphasis on outdoor pursuits and education in appreciation of the natural world as essentials in the well-being of the younger generation added to the holiday population of Snowdonia. The increased ease and speed of access resulting from car travel and improved roads swelled the numbers.

The new industry, for such it was, saved or revived the dying relics of older ones. Old slate mines became tourist attractions far more remunerative than the small remnants of the slate industry that still lingered (and are still carried on today) at Blaenau Ffestiniog and Aberllefenni. The slate railways like the Ffestiniog and Tal-y-llyn lines, largely reconstructed by the volunteer labour of narrow-gauge enthusiasts, began to run again carrying full loads of visitors, and a new hotel on the summit of Snowdon received the vastly increased numbers of passengers brought up by the rack-and-pinion railway built in 1896. The quays and harbours of the coast became busy once more with sailing-craft, not the cargo-carrying schooners and brigs now but the yachts and dinghies of amateur sailors. And with the growing prosperity came new enterprises. The first hydro-electric power station

Public Footpath signs in the national park are the keys to many miles of scenic walking routes. This sign, near Beddgelert, points the walker towards the footpath on the shore of Llyn Dinas.

Like the Ffestiniog Railway, the Tal-y-llyn Railway from Tywyn to beyond the Abergynolwyn originated as a narrow-gauge line carrying slates and is now a major tourist attraction.

was built at Cwm Dyli in 1906, followed by another at Dolgarrog and a third at Maentwrog in 1925. The needs of the growing industrial population in England demanded water from the ample supplies of Snowdonia and reservoirs to maintain the supply. The serious timber shortage made new afforestation essential to the economy, and in 1920 the Forestry Commission acquired its first acreage in Snowdonia.

Not many people had foreseen how rapidly the tourist industry would grow, or how heavy would be these other pressures. Some, however, had perceived that unchecked exploitation of the area could easily ruin it for ever; that the natural beauty and interest which should be the nation's heritage would be lost unless the nation itself took control. The John Dower Report of 1945 which initiated the decisive action of four years later came in the nick of time. And Snowdonia's infinite wealth, immeasurable in terms of money, was preserved for present and future generations by its designation as a national park.

4 The Welsh people and their language

This very short chapter must of necessity fall a long way short of its title. It would be an extremely rash Englishman who proposed to describe the Welsh nation in a book, let alone a chapter; and only a Welshman could write a proper assessment of the Welsh language. All that is intended here is to sketch in a background to the people the visitor will meet and talk to – and hear talking among themselves – when he comes into Snowdonia National Park.

The discovery that the Welsh are a different people from the English often comes as more of a surprise to the visitor from England than to an American or Continental tourist. The Englishman tends to think of the people of Wales as British, like himself, with an amusing and inexplicable preference for talking in a very odd language instead of in his own tongue which they can all speak when they want to. In fact, the language is an outward symbol of a real distinction, old but persisting, between the Anglo-Saxons and the *Cymry*.

Cymry was the name the inhabitants of Snowdonia gave themselves when the centuries of history and prehistory brought the eventual emergence of a Welsh sense of national identity. It can be translated as 'fellow-countrymen', and it has the implication of 'comrades'. Outside the boundaries of Wales they became known as 'Welch', meaning 'other' or 'alien'; and today outsiders call them the Welsh while among themselves they are *y Cymry*. They are different from the English and proud of it. Once, talking to a Welshwoman, I happened to make some casual comment along these lines. She replied at once, and very forcibly, 'Oh, we *are* different – you've no idea *how* different!' And that this should be so isn't all that remarkable when you compare English history with Welsh history. A previous chapter of this book has indicated that the successive waves of invasion from across the North Sea had little impact on Wales, though in England they sowed the seeds of the English people. The Welsh remained Welsh when England was

The working hill farms of Snowdonia are often beautifully situated and maintain a way of life established for many generations.

conquered by the Normans and all but lost its ancient language. The culture that steadily developed west of the protecting mountain barrier, and the language of its poetry and literature, have old and deep roots and their inheritors guard them jealously. The enthusiasm that produces the National Eisteddfod, the festival of music, poetry, and literature held each year at a different Welsh centre, is evidence of the deep feeling for cultural tradition; but it also pervades the whole fabric of social life.

Welsh people have a long historical memory. Edmund Vale in *The World of Wales* tells how in the 1930s he met an old Welsh lady who, learning that he was an Englishman, exclaimed in Welsh 'Dear me! The old English! Remember Morfa Rhuddlan!' She was remembering an eighth-century battle when raiding Saxons massacred Welsh opponents in the marsh of Rhuddlan. It's impossible to imagine an Englishwoman meeting a Dutchman and at once recalling the seventeenth-century Dutch raid into the Medway when towns and villages and many ships were destroyed – indeed, she would probably never have heard of it. In the background of the national consciousness, too, is the knowledge that

when Saxon England had reverted to paganism Wales was still a stronghold of Christianity. The deeds of half a dozen heroes of those shadowy days have perhaps coalesced into the equally shadowy figure of Arthur, the archetypal Christian champion whose last great battle against the pagan hosts was fought in Cwm Tregalan (SH 610535) below Snowdon, and whose sword Excalibur was cast by the faithful Bedwyr (Sir Bedivere) into the dark waters of Llyn Llydaw; an old legend tells us that King Arthur's counsellor-wizard Merlin made his first appearance at Dinas Emrys, two miles up the Gwynant Valley from Beddgelert (SH 606492).

A Welshman of Snowdonia, with his intense love of country and sense of separate nationality, is unlikely to think of himself as living in a national park. He is a man of Gwynedd and the mountains and valleys are the mountains and valley of Gwynedd. But it would be a great mistake to think that Snowdonia National Park is something separate from the Welsh who live in it – on the contrary, they run it. The Park Authority is a Committee of Gwynedd County Council, and the wardens who patrol the park and maintain it are all Welshmen living in the area. When the visitor enters it he will encounter another Welsh tradition that has never lost its continuity: the tradition of hospitality. The people of the north in Wales are shyer with strangers than those of the south; they don't wear their hearts on their sleeves. But no people in the world are more ready to respond to a friendly approach, and once that is made you'll find a welcome of genuine warmth in the valleys – and in the mountains – of Snowdonia.

The National Eisteddfod of Wales, held each year in a different area, requires the erection of big stones – like these at Llanrwst in the Conwy Valley – for the Bardic Circle.

Many incomers taking up residence in Wales have found little difficulty in learning to speak and read Welsh. Contrary to appearances, it isn't as hard to acquire as many European languages and much easier for a foreigner to learn than English. Being a phonetic language, there are no inconsistencies of pronunciation like those presented by *tough*, *bough*, *dough*, *cough* and *through*, so that once you know the sounds of the vowels (which include *y* and *w*) you are well on the way to speaking a Welsh word so that a Welshman will understand it. On the other hand, the language has none of the roots from which English words have grown, though a few nouns show their derivation from the days of the Roman occupation : *eglwys* (Church) from *ecclesia*, for instance, and *pont* (bridge) from *pons*. There are also one or two consonantal sounds that most English people find difficult.

There are many textbooks for those who want to learn Welsh (one of them calls itself, riskily, *Welsh In A Fortnight!*) and it is not proposed to do more here than provide the visitor to the national park with some idea of how place-names are pronounced – a desirable piece of knowledge when you are asking your way. One of the handiest guides to this is Vale's key sentence:

Though funny calves moo gaily,

which, spelt in Welsh fashion, would be something like:

Ddo ffynu cafs mw geli,

though not precisely. Armed with a memorization of those equivalents you are ready for most Welsh place-names except those including *ch* and *ll*. The Scottish *loch* is a guide to the first and for the second the usual tip is to put your tongue immediately above your teeth and breathe out; most English folk find it simpler to make an 'h' sound before the *l* – *hl*.

Many Welsh-learners find it hard to master the mutations. These are a nuisance and not easily to be explained in a short space. It must suffice here to note that nouns and adjectives in place-names can change their initial letters according to certain rules of Welsh grammar, so that the word for 'bridge', for instance, will be 'pont' in Pont-y-pant but 'bont' in Bont-ddu, while the adjective 'bach' (small) becomes 'fach' in the name Glyder Fach. Welshmen

don't drop their voices at the ends of words and sentences as the English do but give full value to all the syllables. *Y Glyder Fach*, when spoken, should have the same emphasis and nearly the same vowel-sounds as 'the mid-air lark'; the *y*, it will be noticed, is pronounced 'uh'.

For pronunciation practice, try reading aloud the place-name components which, with their meanings, are given at the end of this book. For greeting a Welshman when you set out for a walk in the park, try a Welsh 'good morning', which is *bore da*. Say 'boh-reh dah' and you won't be far wrong.

Harlech Castle, perhaps the most romantically situated of all Welsh castles, has also the most spacious views from its battlements.

5 Wildlife in Snowdonia

The ecology of a region more than 800 square miles in area, whose habitats vary from coastal dunes to bare mountaintops 3,000 feet above the sea, has obviously to be greatly condensed in a book of this nature. I have chosen to mention the plants, creatures, and habitats most likely to be seen by any observant visitor to Snowdonia National Park, omitting many rarities mainly of interest to the dedicated botanist or ornithologist. For literature giving more detailed information, inquire at the National Park Information Centres or the Nature Conservancy Council in Bangor.

Dividing the chapter into four regions – upper mountain, moorland and lake, river and woodland, and coast – is convenient but perhaps needs a warning: many species occur in more regions than one, and some of the birds range through all of them at different seasons.

To begin with the plants of the high mountaintops, most of these are survivors from the end of the Ice Age and succeed in growing here because conditions for part of the year resemble arctic or alpine conditions. For instance, on the ridge of the Carneddau, in winter a good imitation of arctic tundra, you find woolly-hair moss, dwarf willow, and the lichen called reindeer moss underfoot in many places. The flowers to be found on and around the highest summits are few but interesting, for they too are survivors of the harder conditions that once prevailed. They bloom before mid-June, and one year I found purple mountain saxifrage, perhaps the commonest of these alpines, flowering in masses in an obscure gully of Lliwedd in February. The pink cushions of moss campion are to be seen on the pale-grey rocks high up on the Glyder precipices, and here too the calcareous rocks support the delicate mountain avens. Rarest of all, and unlikely to be seen unless you are a rock climber, is the Snowdon lily or spiderwort (*Lloydia serotina*) which grows only in Snowdonia and nowhere else in Britain. The cliffs of Twll Du, the Devil's Kitchen (SH 629589), where it may be seen, support many other sorts of arctic-alpine such as rose-root as well

Purple mountain saxifrage.

Snowdon lily.

as typical mountain plants like globe-flower, and the similar habitat on Craig Cau (SH 710125), outlier of Cadair Idris, gives a similar flora – though there is no Snowdon lily here. Some ferns reach right to the rocky tops; beech fern, lady fern, hard fern and the

Tormentil.

broad buckler fern can be found in crevices out of the wind. Wind and sheep are two of the chief enemies the high-mountain plants have to fight against, and where steep crags are well sheltered they thrive. On Craig y Dulyn (SH 697667), at 2,500 ft (763 m) on the east slope of the Carneddau ridge, seventy-five different plant species have been found. Mosses are high climbers, especially the fir clubmoss which gets to the very tops of the mountains, while its brother the easily identifiable stagshorn clubmoss curls its long branched stems on the grassier slopes below.

The high shoulders and slopes carpeted with thin turf where the sheep graze in summer show a gem-like array of small flowers led by the little yellow stars of tormentil, of all flowers the most characteristic of our mountainsides, with the white of heath bedstraw and the blue of heath milkwort providing colour-contrast. Relatively few flowers except the ubiquitous heather are to be found among the volcanic crags of Tryfan, and the rocky humps of the Rhinog – another acid region where heather thrives – are also rather poor in mountain flora, though the mossy saxifrage occurs on Rhinog Fach and above Cwm Moch (SH 665363).

The birds of the upper mountain are less likely to be seen on the Rhinog than on the higher summits and taller crags of the Snowdon group. I saw my first peregrine on Moel Hebog (Hill of the Falcon) (SH 565469) above Beddgelert when we were making the first ascent of a rock climb on the eastern precipice. I was crouched on a small ledge below an overhang, belaying the leader's rope while he struggled with unseen difficulties overhead, when something swept downwards past my ledge with a *whoosh!* like the noise of a rocket. I thought the leader had fallen off and braced myself for the shock. But simultaneously with a reassuring shout from above I saw what looked like a puff of white smoke from a small explosion far down in the cwm below – the drift of feathers as the peregrine struck her prey. A peregrine, they say, swoops at 150 miles an hour, and will strike at birds as big as red grouse or bigger; the puff of feathers I saw probably came from a pigeon. Happily this fine falcon is on the increase and more peregrines are now nesting in the national park. Eagles, of course, do not nest in Snowdonia, though now and then a wanderer (perhaps from Scotland) is reported. The raven may seem a poor substitute, but to see a raven soaring on the thermals is almost as fine a sight as a soaring eagle, and his masterly aerobatics, often to be seen from the summit ridges of Cadair Idris and Snowdon, are fascinating to watch. The wren, only one-seventh the size of the raven, shares his liking for the very highest rocks. Her piercing voice directed into my ear from a cranny two feet away once nearly dislodged me from my holds when I

Peregrine falcon.

Moss campion.

Wren.

Ring ouzel.

Wheatear (cock).

was climbing in a rock chimney at 2,900 ft (885 m) on Glyder Fawr. Like the ravens, wrens stay up here in the winter among the snow and ice, sheltering in miniscule caves as befits their Latin name of *Troglodytes*. The chough likes to visit the summits in summer, when I've seen them on the top of Moel-yr-Ogof (SH 556478) looking very handsome and quite unmistakable with their long red bills and red legs. They nest in crags and quarries lower down the mountain and are most exhilarating to watch in flight. Until very recently their numbers in Snowdonia were declining, but current reports indicate that here in the national park, almost the only place in Britain where they nest and breed inland, they are at least holding their own.

Kestrels and buzzards are bound to be in sight at some time during a visit to Snowdonia. The kestrel, known in northern Britain as 'windhover', hangs motionless head-to-wind on the lookout for the field mice and voles that are its prey. In sunlight its chestnut upper plumage shows plainly. Sun on the buzzard's gold-brown feathers as it slowly wheels has more than once caused it to be mistaken for a golden eagle. Neither kestrel nor buzzard haunt the high ridges so persistently as the raven – or, for that matter, as the herring gull, whose greedy eye and incongruous webbed feet can be seen at close quarters on Crib Goch or Yr Wyddfa whenever you sit down to open your sandwich-box. The ring ouzel with his white cravat is so shy of company that it's something of a triumph to spot one; though often to be seen in river gorges he likes the high rocks and nests there, so spring is the time to see him up aloft.

The sheep-runs below the crags are alive with small birds in spring and early summer, meadow pipits and wheatears skipping from one hillside boulder to another. The wheatear with his flashing white rump is a particular joy and is numerous throughout the mountains of the national park; the cock's back is slate-grey, the hen's brown. And another joy in spring is the skylark's song. One doesn't think of skylarks as mountain birds, yet from April to June on the 3,000-foot ridges of the Carneddau you walk below a continuous avenue of lark-song; handed on, so to speak, from one spiralling lark to the next.

The ponies that may be seen roaming wild on the flanks of the Carneddau and on mountainsides farther south, notably on Arenig and Aran, are semi-domesticated and can't be classed as wildlife. Nor

'Wild' ponies, like these on the northern Carneddau slopes, are part of a hill-farmer's stock but are allowed to graze freely on the mountains.

can the fine stag I once encountered on a day of drifting mist, trying to find its way down into Cwm Eigiau; it had escaped from a private estate. Red deer were once common in Snowdonia, as is indicated by the name Llwybr Carw (the Deer's Path) on the Devil's Kitchen crags in Cwm Idwal, but the last one was hunted down well before the end of the eighteenth century. The feral goats, of which there are several herds in the national park, are descendants of semi-domesticated stock but must surely be regarded as 'wild' by now. They are to be seen among the higher rocks on Tryfan and the Glyder, Rhinog, Rhobell Fawr, and Cadair Idris, but they are elusive animals and change their haunts frequently. The senior billygoats are often magnificent beasts with great horns like ibex, and when they pose on a rocky skyline as they're fond of doing they look most picturesque. A herd of ten or a dozen is usual, though on an early spring day some years ago I counted forty-two goats, including a number of kids, disporting themselves in the wild cwm below Bwlch y Ddwy-Glyder on the south flank of Glyder Fach (SH 652582).

The hill farmers tolerate the goats though these encroach to some extent on the sheep pastures. The farmer at Gwern-gof uchaf farm below Tryfan told me that the Tryfan goats are useful to him because they eat the succulent plants that grow on the ledges and cracks of the steep rock-faces, thus removing temptation from the sheep who – less sure-footed – might try to graze there and fall to their deaths.

No farmer likes or tolerates the other large (and truly wild) animal of the park, the fox. Welshmen will tell you that there are two kinds of fox: the *milgi* or big grey mountain fox and the *corgi*, the smaller red lowland fox. Zoologists don't agree. Certainly the fox I saw fleeting up a boulder-scree high on the flank of Cnicht was large and greyish, but I've often seen very red foxes just as high up among the crags. They are hunted and trapped persistently, for they are rapacious robbers of poultry and – so the farmers maintain – young lambs, but they are still plentiful on the mountains.

Wide areas of undulating grass moorland between 1,000 and 2,000 feet above the sea flank the mountains of Snowdonia National Park on the east, extending southward from the Denbigh moors and Mynydd Hiraethog (not within the park boundary) through the Migneint and the Bala uplands to the hills north of the Dyfi. Some of it is in course of afforestation, and the drainage of bogs for conifer-planting is tending to reduce the habitat of birds such as dunlin and golden plover, which are becoming rare. On the other hand, the little trees of new forestry foster a new ecology, affording nesting cover for meadow pipit and whinchat and the interesting short-eared owl, and homes for mice and other small mammals which are the food of owl and kestrel. On this terrain the merlin, the smallest British falcon, is also likely to be seen making its

Fox.

dashing low-level raids.

Untouched heather moorland has a rather greater variety of birds, plants and animals. On the Migneint (SH 780430), the big area of bog and heath north of Arenig Fawr, red grouse and blackcock nest as do kestrel and buzzard. When you walk on the Migneint you are sure to put up a snipe and see it whizz away on its rapid zigzag flight, and you are equally sure to see the wheatears and pipits that inhabit the rocky combs that heave themselves above the moorland. The occasional heron will be looking for frogs and fish in the marshy streams, and higher up the same streams the miniature cascades are the haunt of dipper and grey wagtail.

The centre of the Migneint is about the wildest place you can find in the whole of the national park, despite the unfenced road that crosses it from Llan Ffestiniog to Ysbyty Ifan, and its little reed-fringed lake, Llyn Serw, has an uncanny way of appearing from nowhere when you come upon it and vanishing again as soon as you leave its boggy shore. Here as on the other Migneint lakes – Llyn Arenig Fach, Llyn y Dywarchen, Llyn Conwy, and Llynau Gamallt – you are likely to see in spring a pair of nesting mallard or teal, and in summer a common sandpiper or two. Stretching away on either side of the Crimea road-pass above Dolwyddelan is a similar moorland area with two lakes, Llyn Newydd and Llyn Bowydd.

Apart from the small creatures that scuttle among the heather-roots – short-tailed vole, fieldmouse, pygmy shrew – the fox is to be looked for wherever there are open slopes of rock and heather, and the brown hare on the grassier moorland. Grass snakes, up to three feet long and harmless, like the wetter parts of the moor and are perfectly capable of swimming across the meandering streams of the marshes. The adder, with its blunt triangle of head and thick body, prefers drier places such as a south-facing pile of rocks. The only British poisonous snake, its chief anxiety when you approach it is to get away and hide; but in early spring its senses are dull after the long hibernation, it can't move quickly, and it might strike to defend itself if your boot treads near it.

For me the characteristic plant of the moorlands is the bog myrtle, sometimes called sweet gale, whose leaves bruised between the fingers produce a scent evoking the pleasures of summer solitude among the hills. Higher and drier than the myrtle grow the two sorts of heather, the bell heather making its summer display first before the ling or Scottish

Whinchat.

heather covers the hill-slopes with pale mauve-pink. The brighter pink of another heather, the cross-leaved heath, also shows itself in late summer but in moister places. Bog asphodel's brilliant yellow spikes also appear in wet locations, often near the common spotted orchid, and the damp-loving sundew and butterwort, both insectivorous plants, will probably be growing not far away. The round-leaved sundew (*Drosera rotundifolia*) is common everywhere in Snowdonia but long-leaved sundew (*Drosera intermedia*) is rarer and a good find if you spot it.

The moorland lakes are usually shallow, and perhaps the commonest flower to see near them, or often in them, is the bogbean, whose pale pink flower-heads stand up above a raft of floating leaves in early summer. Water-lilies both white and yellow are to be seen on some of the upland tarns, as on Llyn Cwm-mynach (SH 678237) on the eastern flank of the Rhinog, which is also rich in other aquatic plants. Small trout may be found in such lakes, but the deeper mountain lakes hold more attraction for the fisherman; Llyn Edno (SH 663497) at 1,800 ft (549 m) north east of Cnicht is noted for trout, and so is Ffynnon Lloer behind the eastern shoulder of Pen yr Oleu Wen in the Carneddau.

The bigger lakes down in the valleys are, with few exceptions, angling lakes and are kept stocked with fish. Llyn Myngul (Tal-y-llyn lake), Llyn Dinas and Cwellyn near Snowdon, and Llyn Crafnant in the Carneddau – to take four examples – have their fishy population watched over by the angling associations. One lake, however, contains a fish that antedates by far all the others. Llyn Tegid (Bala lake) is the home of the remarkable gwyniad, a fish that established itself there at the close of the Ice Age and has remained ever since; it is rather like a small herring to look at and occurs nowhere else in Britain. Grayling, a rare fish in Snowdonia, are also in this lake but are said to have been deliberately introduced. Llyn Tegid's water-birds are not numerous considering it is the largest natural lake in the national park. All the same, you may see mallard and pochard, and towards the quieter south-western end of the lake herons fish; here too is the breeding-place of a number of smaller birds including sedge warbler and reed bunting. Tal-y-llyn lake, sixteen miles from Bala and in the same geological fault-line, has more birds to show in winter, when whooper swan, tufted duck, goldeneye and many others come to feed.

Llyn Tecwyn-isaf below the foothills of the Rhinog mountains.

Llyn Tecwyn Isaf (SH 630370), in woodland surroundings at the foot of the northern Rhinog, merits a small paragraph to itself for its unique charm. Coot and dabchick are its chief frequenters, pottering round the shady margins where marsh St John's wort and water-lilies grow. It is reached by very narrow lanes from the village of Llandecwyn, near Penrhyndeudraeth.

Farther north below the eastern ridges of Snowdon lie two lakes quite close together, either of which could claim to be the most beautiful lake in the national park – despite the fact that the A498 runs along the shores of both. Llyn Dinas has sea-trout and salmon for the fisherman but its real treasure is its placid beauty spreading from the wooded crags above the lakeside road to distant mountains beyond its farther shore. Its neighbour Llyn Gwynant (SH 645520) is populous in summer with canoes, a sailing-dinghy or two and a host of gaily coloured tents at the lake-head; pretty enough but not Llyn Gwynant at its best. That comes on a clear cold day in November, perhaps, when the lakeside road is quiet and the crags of the Glyder far above show their first powdering of snow against the blue; when the great mountainsides arch down in russet

and gold to meet their reflections in the still water. Then you could say with truth that Snowdonia National Park can have nothing to show more beautiful than this.

In the far north of the national park the Afon Goch, rising in a bare mountain-glen of the Carneddau, hurls itself over the sheer 200 ft (61 m) cliff of the Aber Falls to rattle down two miles of wooded valley to the sea (SH 669700). In the far south of the park the Afon Dysynni pursues a peaceful and meandering course for fourteen miles without a single waterfall, curling through the widening flats north of Tywyn to reach its almost landlocked estuary at Broad Water. These two extremes exemplify the variety of the many rivers and streams in Snowdonia. The most typical little river is the mountain stream that tumbles from its birthplace on moorland or mountainside to cascade excitingly through mossy woodlands to the estuary valley, with countless small waterfalls and pools on the way. Ganllwyd, on the A470 six miles north of Dolgellau, is a good base for exploring this sort of river, having on the west the delightful path leading up through the ancient woodland of the Coed Ganllwyd Nature Reserve (SH 726244) with its ferns and

Aber Falls (Rhaeadr Fawr) at the head of a wooded valley below the northern Carneddau.

mosses to the Rhaeadr Ddu, and on the east beyond the bridge over the Mawddach the newer forest in which are hidden two very scenic waterfalls, Pistyll Cain (SH 736275) and Rhaeadr Mawddach (SH 737276).

Salmon and sea-trout come up-river as far as Rhaeadr Mawddach, apparently unaffected by the operations of the Gwynfynydd Gold Mine just above. By the pools and skipping about the rocks below the falls are the wagtails, the pied wagtail

Dipper.

more abundant than the grey wagtail, whose lemon-yellow underside and blue-grey upper parts make him one of the handsomest of small birds. Dippers are often seen, flying fast and low close to the stream or doing their continuous bobbing on a rock just above the surface. Each dipper has his own 'beat' of stream which he defends pugnaciously, and his nest will be somewhere on that beat; in a cranny of the stream-side rocks, under a bridge if there is one, or even behind a waterfall. His food is aquatic insects, and if you are lucky you may see him swimming after them below the surface, using his wings as propellors. He is shaped rather like an outsize wren, with dark-brown topsides and a conspicuous white bib.

Ferns and mosses thrive in the damp places by the beds of streams such as these, and the river gorges of southern Meirionnydd have long been famous among botanists for such plants as the rarer spleenworts, bladder fern, and hard shield fern. The long-celebrated Torrent Walk two miles east of Dolgellau is a comparatively easy gorge in which to look out for them, and so is the little ravine of the Dolgoch Falls (SH 652043) above the Dolgoch station of the Tal-y-llyn narrow-gauge railway, another old-

Welsh poppy.

established beauty spot. Among the flowers, the yellow Welsh poppy (*Mecanopsis cambrica*) is rarer in the south than it is nearer Snowdon, though it is to be found in Cwm Cywarch above Dinas Mawddwy as well as in Cwm Cau on Cadair Idris.

In the fine river-gorge of the Afon Cynfal the scenery tends to distract attention from the details of plant and animal life, for it is as impressive as any in Britain. You can descend into it from the village of Llan Ffestiniog and take a path along the steep side of the gorge, whence your views of dippers and wagtails tend to be bird's-eye views. If you follow the public footpaths upstream until you can walk no farther you come to the precipitous cleft down which the Cynfal River comes plunging in a series of six waterfalls, a total height of 300 ft (92 m).

Where the streams run through valleys wider and less gloomy than the deep-carved gorges the ecology of woodland, plant, and river is at its happiest. I am thinking particularly of the Artro River (SH 615285) that flows out of Llyn Cwmbychan and down to the sea at Llanbedr, for much of the way bordered by ancient woods of sessile oaks and mossy rocks. If you drive up the narrow road from Llanbedr (busy in summer) you'll find one or two picnic sites where you can halt and wander by the riverside, watching the brown trout in the pools and savouring the atmosphere of a stream that is somehow peculiarly *Welsh*. And there will be – as always in the old oakwoods – plenty of woodland birds; various tits, redstart, nuthatch, wood warbler, perhaps a pied flycatcher, in addition to the dippers and wagtails in the river-bed.

The Forestry Commission's conifer plantations that now cover more than twelve per cent of the national park's area are always poorer in birds,

The Mawddach River, seen from the Precipice Walk near Dolgellau, reaches its wide estuary leading to the sea at Barmouth.

In Gwydyr Forest rocky vantage-points rising above the trees make good lookout posts for bird-watchers.

animals and plants than are the deciduous woodlands. Yet they have encouraged some birds that were previously rare visitors to stay and breed in Snowdonia, and redpoll and siskin have now been breeding in these forests for some years. To see what this comparatively recent habitat has to show the best way is to make the round of a forest trail; the Gwydyr Forest Trail that starts from near Betws-y-Coed, for example. Besides blackbirds and thrushes and the three common kinds of tit, you are likely to see stonechat, goldcrest, jay, magpie, and woodcock, and perhaps siskin and redpoll. The forest clearings outside the gloom of the conifers have a different population and here you would look out for willow warbler, pied flycatcher, redstart and wren.

The twilight of the conifers attracts some of the less common animals, especially if there are crags and rock outcrops under the trees as there are in the Gwydyr Forest. The polecat, so darkly furred that it looks quite black, is numerous in the national park but not easy to identify because you usually see no more than the flash of movement that heralds its disappearance. Considerably bigger than a stoat, with a long sinuous body, it is a nocturnal hunter but will hunt in daytime in a dark forest. The dark-brown pine marten, which William Condry calls 'Snowdonia's most distinguished mammal', is much rarer than the polecat and very few people have seen one; but a conifer forest is as likely a place as any to become one of the few.

A rather unusual sighting of a pine marten was made recently by a rock-climber, looking down

The striking outline of the Bird Rock (Craig yr Aderyn) in the Dysynni Valley near Tywyn.

from the vertical rock wall, where he was clinging, into the deep crannies of the boulder slope beneath him. This was at Coed Tremadog (SH 575407), one of the Nature Conservancy's ten woodland reserves in the park and differing from the others in that it consists mostly of a fine scarp-face of high dolerite cliffs, one of the most popular climbing-grounds in Britain. The climbers share these cliffs with nesting kestrels, ravens, and jackdaws, but careful control of access (a permit is required) has preserved the wildlife and the variety of lime-loving plants that grow on the dolerite ledges and the boulder-scree below.

Coed Tremadog is not an easy place to visit, but two of the woodland reserves are particularly suitable for family parties. Neither of them requires a permit. The first is Coed Llyn Mair (SH 666417), part of the Coedydd Maentwrog (Maentwrog Woodlands) which were acquired by the National Trust and the North Wales Naturalists' Trust. A good way to walk the short nature trail that has been laid out here is to arrive at Tan-y-Bwlch station by way of the Ffestiniog Railway from Porthmadog, thus beginning with a ride on one of the old slate rail lines. The trail starts from the station and winds

Polecat.

downhill beside a woodland stream. Besides the
trees and flowers, the birds you might see include
great tits and blue tits, pied flycatcher, jay,
treecreeper, nuthatch and great spotted
woodpecker. There is a helpful explanatory leaflet
for this trail; and the nesting-boxes placed here and
there by the Nature Conservancy wardens could be
a useful guide if you want to encourage birds in
your garden. At the foot of the trail, where there is a
very pretty lakeside picnic site, there are
blackheaded gulls on Llyn Mair (Mary's lake)
(SH 653412) as well as mallard and coot.

The other woodland walk is less sophisticated, an
old path rising and falling across the slopes of
primeval sessile oakwoods half a mile north of
Maentwrog village. To start it, go 300 yards
eastward along the A487 from the Oakeley Arms
hotel at Tan-y-Bwlch, then fork left on a narrow lane;
another 300 yards along the lane there is a gate and
a 'Nature Reserve' sign on the left. There are two
very pretty streams to be crossed, each with its
waterfall, and it is possible to follow the path up to
the remote Elizabethan manor house of Dduallt and
return by a higher route. In addition to the birds
mentioned in the previous paragraph you could – if
you were lucky – see all three British woodpeckers
– great spotted, lesser spotted, and green – for they
all nest in this woodland. May is the time for flowers
in the broad-leaved woods, and here the mossy
slopes are carpeted with wood anemone, wood
sorrel, violet, primrose and bluebell. Coedydd
Maentwrog harbour fox and badger; but to see
them you would need to be walking up-wind and
very quietly.

Estuaries are coastal territory, at least as far
inland as they are tidal. But one haunt and breeding-
place of sea birds in the national park is unique – an

inland rock-face overlooking farm meadow-land a good five miles from the sea. The Bird Rock (Craig yr Aderyn) stands in the Dysynni Valley two miles south west of the ruined fortress of Castell y Bere (SH 642068), a striking conical peak nearly 800 feet above the flat valley bottom, its frontal cliff a sheer precipice. For the past two centuries cormorants have nested on the ledges of the precipice. Probably they chose this inland crag because there are no rocky nesting-places for them on the long sandy coast between Aberdyfi and Barmouth, where for a long time big shoals of herring and mackerel were common. With the departure of the

The Dwyryd estuary, seaward continuation of the Vale of Ffestiniog, is the haunt of many kinds of waders and sea birds.

shoals the numbers of nesting cormorants declined; but there are still two or three dozen pairs to be seen there in April and May. You can get to Craig yr Aderyn by taking the lane northward from Bryncrug, two and a half miles from Tywyn.

The estuaries of Mawddach and Glaslyn and Dyfi teem with birds of all kinds, not only the waders whose customary habitat they are but also mountain birds, sea birds, and birds of passage. In that excellent little book *Birdwatching in Snowdonia*, by E Breeze Jones and G E Thomas, the estuaries are described as air termini for bird travellers, and though the rarer avian tourists are most likely to be seen in winter there is great variety at all times of year. Redshank, curlew, lapwing, grey and golden plover, dunlin, common sandpiper and ringed plover, prod for food in the shallows while red-breasted merganser fish farther out. Kingfishers favour these wider rivers and estuaries; a kingfisher used regularly to dive from the mast of my dinghy moored near the seaward end of the Glaslyn estuary. And in the reedy *traeth* between Trwyn Penrhyn and Porthmadog harbour a community of swans – twenty-two at the last count – nests and thrives.

Oystercatchers like the flat sands of the wide estuaries, where they can run after the falling tide and catch the shellfish before these have time to close up, but in calm weather they can be seen on the open sea-beaches, trotting along the water's edge with dunlin and sanderling. And here of course are the gulls. The largest gull in sight is likely to be a herring gull, though the larger and rarer great black-backed gull (two and a half feet from bill to tail) might be seen, for it nests inland in small numbers in this area. The noisy blackheaded gulls are nearly always to be seen and heard; they too have inland nesting-places, notably at the Trawsfynydd lake reservoir (their biggest colony) and beside the small lakes in the higher clearings of the Gwydyr Forest. Most of the others nest either on the shingle or on the grassy dunes behind the beaches. For these the two Nature Reserves on the coast of the national park offer protection.

One of the few surviving breeding colonies of little terns in North Wales is to be found just outside the national park boundary at Tywyn. The site is fenced every spring and wardened by the Royal Society for the Protection of Birds throughout the breeding season.

The dune-lands of the north Meironnydd coast provide a type of landscape totally unlike anything else in the national park. It's worth getting the necessary permit from the Nature Conservancy just to be able to wander for a while in the other-world surroundings of Morfa Harlech or Morfa Dyffryn with their miniature pinkish-brown mountains and valleys where unusual plants and flowers grow. Marsh helleborine and other kinds of orchid grow in these valleys as does the creeping willow and on the drier flanks of the dunes burnet rose, lady's bedstraw, and rest-harrow flourish, among others. Several species of butterfly and moth live among the flowers and dragonflies flit across the little pools. The Morfa Harlech Reserve, with its 1,214 acres of sand flats and marsh and dune, is the better of the two for bird observation. Among the common nesting birds here are mallard, shelduck, oystercatcher, redshank, ringed plover, curlew and lapwing, and there is a colony of blackheaded gulls.

In the Morfa Harlech Reserve there is a sand dune

Oystercatcher.

Little tern.

so high that the old Ordnance Survey maps used to
mark its height – 65 feet, if I remember it correctly.
From this tiny summit on the sea coast one can look
across to the mountains of Snowdonia and take in at a
single glance all the different strata of habitat and
scenery that go to make up Snowdonia National
Park: coast, estuary, river, woodland, mountain
stream, moorland, open hillside, mountain crest. It
would be odd, I think, if one didn't feel very thankful
that all this has been taken into care, to be
preserved for the interest and enjoyment of future
generations.

6 The national park today

No one nowadays disputes the value to the nation of the national parks. There is a growing awareness that conservation is essential, not only to thousands of wild species in danger of extinction but also to the survival of the human race itself. Moreover, the value of the parks increases with every acre of Britain's dwindling surface that is sealed-off by the proliferation of motorways, airports, and industrial estates. Recreation in the form of open-air pursuits has also been recognized as essential to the health of the community in the last two decades, and this too requires the open unspoiled countryside which the parks provide. So while one aim of Snowdonia National Park is conservation, another aim is the furtherance of recreation. The achievement of both these aims, which are not always easy to reconcile, demands efficient organization, careful planning,

Moel Hebog, Hill of the Hawk, seen above Nant Colwyn in winter.

A riverside walk near Beddgelert.

and many and varied kinds of hard work.

The Snowdonia National Park Authority functions as a Committee of Gwynedd County Council. It is funded by Central Government (seventy-five per cent) on the advice of the Countryside Commission and by the County Council (twenty-five per cent). As guardian of the park the Authority has the difficult task of balancing the needs of conservation and recreation with the needs of local people who live and work within the park. These demands can conflict, and calls for 'bread before beauty' are often heard when the Authority seeks to prevent unsuitable developments, projects which might harm the environment but would on the other hand provide jobs for local people in an area which has a very high unemployment rate. But tourism, a major employer in the park, relies on the quality of the landscape which visitors come to see.

The Snowdonia National Park Committee is the local planning authority for the national park and as such can lay down statutory long-term planning policies for it. By using its development control powers is can ensure that proposals for development accord with these policies, which are aimed as striking a balance between the conflicting demands made on the park, and it is able to exercise influence on such things as the design of new housing, the siting of additional car parks and the initiation of commercial enterprises.

For instance, a private individual may acquire a disused mine with the idea of developing it as a tourist attraction for his own profit. In considering such a proposal the Committee will weigh the advantages – an extra tourist attraction, the provision of local employment – against the possible disadvantages which could include the building of an access road and the provision of a car park, either of which could constitute an eyesore in a scenic neighbourhood. If it was decided that the development would be detrimental to the natural scenery, the Committee would employ its powers in opposing the scheme.

This illustrates one of the National Park Authority's dilemmas. There are others. If the conservation of scenery and its enjoyment are important to the nation, so is the national need for water and power, whose values are more tangible and immediate. If the nation decides the need is proven, the Authority has to accept the reservoirs and power stations that result from these essential needs and make the best of them; though it does have a considerable say in what they are to look like when they are sited and built. A big sheet of water like the Llyn Celyn Reservoir (beneath which lies the drowned village of Tryweryn) is sightly enough when full to the brim but ugly when it is half empty; but laybys and picnic places at the lakeside provide some compensation. The dam at Llyn Stwlan (SH 665445), 1,500 feet up in the heart of the Moelwyn mountains, was widely execrated when it was built for the pumped storage scheme of the Tan-y-grisiau Power Station near Blaenau Ffestiniog and it is still an eyesore; but many people who visit the national park take an interest in power stations and dams, and today the combined trip by Ffestiniog Railway and bus to Llyn Stwlan is popular with visitors. Even the atomic power station at Trawsfynydd (SH 690370), a presence to be deplored anywhere let alone in a national park, has added one amenity that benefits wildlife, for an island in its artificial lake provides a rare inland nesting-place for the great black-backed gull.

From time to time application is made to institute large mineral-mining projects in Snowdonia. Gold, copper, lead, manganese and others are still there, but the richness of the ore-lodes is extremely

The extensive forests of Coed y Brenin seen from the start of the Precipice Walk above Dolgellau.

variable and they are so uncertainly distributed in the national park that small mines are today unremunerative, and only a vast mechanized mining project disgorging huge mountains of spoil would be economically viable. One such project has been successfully resisted; and with the resultant permanent damage to the park so inevitable others are unlikely to be supported.

Many people dislike the dark conifer forests of Snowdonia National Park and have been known to ask why they were ever allowed. Forestry became a vital British industry in the 1920s before the national park was thought of. Snowdonia's unforested uplands and poor soil was then the obvious place for plantings, and conifers were used because no other kind of tree is so marketable or grows so quickly. The early plantings were made without regard to environmental considerations, sometimes in rectangular blocks as in the Beddgelert Forest, which was one of the first to be planted. These initial plantations are now coming to maturity and the trees are being felled for replanting to take place. Since the first afforestation much has changed in Snowdonian forestry and the Sitka spruce that makes the dark-looking forests is by no means the

National park wardens
consolidating a footpath
on Snowdon.

only conifer to be seen. Scots pine, Douglas fir,
western red cedar, western hemlock and larch are
to be found in all the forests; plantations are made in
harmony with the contours of the hills and their
shapes; and it is now the general practice to plant
deciduous trees as well as conifers and to diversify
the edges of plantations with a variety of
hardwoods. The Forestry Commission within
Snowdonia National Park has brought its forests into
line with the aims of the Park Authority, providing
waymarked trails, picnic sites, and a Forestry Camp
Site near Beddgelert; orienteering clubs use the
forests for their sport. But the conifers are still alien
to Snowdonia and always will be, and it can only be
matter for regret that current economic pressures
are almost certain to lead to pressure for their
further proliferation.

Dealing with the problems of encroachment and
development and its assimilation is only one of the
Park Authority's tasks. The visitor will see plenty of
evidence of its continuing work of maintenance.
Most obvious, perhaps, is the reconstruction and
consolidating of paths and ways of access, made
necessary by the impact of 'human erosion'.

It is a curious circumstance that one of the most
active agents of erosion since the Ice Age carved
the mountains is man. The great pale scars of his
paths can be seen on mountainsides from many
miles away and his pleasure-seeking tread mashes
the valley tracks into bog. Sheer weight of numbers
is responsible for this. In 1985 it was estimated that
1,500 walkers and 1,000 train passengers reach
Snowdon summit on a fine day in summer; during
the peak period from 1.30 to 3 pm the summit may

have over 1,000 people on it at any one time. Thus the rocky cone of Yr Wyddfa with its big cairn undergoes as much trampling as a city pavement, and must be strengthened and reinforced with well-defined paths if it is not eventually to be worn away. In 1979, the Snowdon Management Scheme was started, funded largely by the Countryside Commission, to tackle the most seriously eroded areas, and since then the national park maintenance gangs work throughout the year maintaining and rebuilding the paths on Snowdon.

On the less populous but popular smaller mountain, Cnicht, you can see plainly how in many places the normal route, a grassy path twenty-five years ago, has had its surface of turf entirely removed, leaving awkward bare rock and causing walkers to make a by-pass route – which in its turn will become eroded. On Cnicht as on other mountains nature's own agents, rain and frost and wind, have seized on man's surface breakage to aid in speeding-up their otherwise slow but relentless process.

For the Warden Service of Snowdonia National Park the maintenance of paths is one of many responsibilities. There are nine Wardens, each with his own section of the park to patrol, and all are ready with help or information for the visitor. If you meet a Warden on the hills you will recognize him by his dark-blue jersey with a red stripe and by his badge showing the national park symbol; when there is doubt about a route or the weather his advice should always be followed. In the valleys a Warden's vehicle can be recognized by the Park badge on its white bodywork. His jobs include helping and advising farmers, caring for woodlands, inspecting and maintaining stiles, taking part in rescue parties, and keeping a watchful eye on the wildlife and plant life. And of course the paths, which with numbers of visitors increasing every year present a continuing problem. The paths in a Warden's section may be steep and wooded, like the little path mounting to Llyn Elsi (SH 783553) from Betws-y-Coed; or easy but narrow like the scenic Precipice Walk path (SH 744213) above Dolgellau; or a crag-clinging trail like the upper part of the Miners' Track on Snowdon, which has had to be extensively built up and protected. Some may deplore the artificial strengthening of the old paths, but it is essential – on Snowdon and Cadair Idris particularly – that reasonable means of access should be established and maintained.

Access in a slightly different sense can sometimes present a problem for the Wardens and the Park Authority. There have been instances where hill farmers, perturbed by the breaking-down of walls or fences by thoughtless walkers, have resolved to ban visitors from their upper pastures. Then only tactful negotiation, aided by the excellent relations maintained between Warden and farmer, can save the situation. Within recent years the Park Authority has averted the danger of complete exclusion of walkers from the Aran mountains above Bala, by a courtesy footpath agreement which gives access to both summits.

The extensive organization behind the Wardens has to deal with a great many other matters besides access agreements. One major undertaking is the Residential Field Study Centre at Plas Tan-y-Bwlch, where throughout the year fifty or more courses are available to students and others; the maintenance of this splendidly situated eighteenth-century mansion and its surrounding gardens and woodland, with the necessary catering and accommodation, requires a special staff as does the programme of lectures and field expeditions. Another is Llyn Tegid, Bala lake, where the National Park Authority's Lake Warden

The start of the Pyg track up Snowdon, with Crib Goch in the distance. Erosion has made it necessary to repair some mountain paths very solidly.

controls the boating and fishing. In addition the Authority staffs and maintains the seven National Park Information Centres, prepares and publishes the literature and guide leaflets for distribution at the Centres, manages the toilets and car parks and adjacent information boards, arranges the Snowdon Sherpa bus service which in summer provides much-needed local transport for walkers, fosters educational opportunities through its Youth and Schools Liaison Officer, and organizes guided walks and talks programmes at centres throughout the park. Through its Forestry Officer the Park Authority exercises a continuing and improving influence on the woodland landscapes of the park. In addition to planning the landscaping of new forestry plantations (in conjunction with the Forestry Commission), the Forestry Officer is concerned with the re-establishment of broad-leaved woodlands. This important work, which might be called rehabilitation, requires the co-operation of the farmer in fencing relict woodland or making part of his land available for planting, which is mainly of oak. In this way the oakwoods, natural to Snowdonia and so much richer in flora and fauna than the conifer forests, are being given a chance to recover a little – a very little – of the ground lost by centuries of destruction.

Two instances, chosen from many, will show the wide range of the work with which the National Park Authority is constantly engaged. The first concerns the Agricultural Liaison Officer, another of the Authority's key men. Farmers who wish to apply for Ministry of Agriculture grants for land improvement have first to seek the approval of the Park Authority; this enables the Authority to determine whether or not the improvement will have a damaging effect on the landscape. In one such case the proposed improvements were in an area noted for its scenic beauty and involved the clearance of rough pasture where rock outcrops, patches of bracken, and scrub oaks formed a natural and beautiful part of the landscape. The Agricultural Liaison Officer visited the site and discussed the matter with the farmer. As a result, it was agreed that the farmer would leave untouched the scenic outcrop areas and improve the land between them, which was in any case more accessible to his farm machinery. His grant application was accepted and the rough outcrops with their untouched natural beauty were preserved.

In the second example it is a plant that poses the

A young beech-tree struggles towards the light in a conifer forest.

problem. When ornamental rhododendrons were introduced into Snowdonia by eighteenth-century landowners it was not foreseen that the most vigorous of these, *Rhododendron ponticum*, would spread far and wide across great areas of terrain between sea level and 1,000 feet. For example, this beautiful plant now clothes the steep sides of Aberglaslyn Pass and the craggy slopes above Beddgelert, where it is to be seen in flower about mid-June. Many visitors who enjoy the colourful display condemn the policy that sets out to destroy or restrict it; but there are urgent reasons for this policy. *R. ponticum* is a killer. Because it is extremely poisonous to animals, it has no enemies to keep it in check, and one large bush can produce several million fertile seeds each year. Under its dense shade nothing will grow. When it spreads in a wood, that wood is doomed, for not only the woodland plants but also the tree seedlings die. All the animals, birds, and insects that rely on these plants for food and shelter leave. And as it thrives on the sheep pastures as well, the hill farmers lose valuable grazing. If it is allowed to go on spreading large patches of the national park will become monotonous dark-green shrubberies, totally flowerless for eleven months of the year, and many species of wildlife are likely to vanish from the affected areas. The first stage in the offensive against it was to make a survey of the whole of the park to discover the extent of this disastrous invasion. The second will be to take opposing action; 'will be', because an easy, safe, and completely effective method of controlling *R. ponticum* has yet to be found.

The permanent fund of pleasure, interest, and instruction which is constituted by Snowdonia National Park has been briefly described in this book, and the work that goes into its maintenance hinted at. Most of the active maintenance work is carried out by the Authority's estate workers, but from time to time it may have to employ outside labour. It can also, in the holiday season when more mountain patrols are needed, call on the services of a fluctuating number of voluntary Wardens; usually there are between forty and fifty of these, most of them active hill walkers living in or near the park.

Rhododendron ponticum spreading up the mountainsides at Beddgelert.

Visitors who appreciate the great value of the park to the nation may wish to know of ways in which they can help in its preservation and improvement. For the energetic there is the active

work of the Snowdonia Conservation Volunteers; or where youth groups are concerned the leader can get in touch with the National Park's Youth and Schools Liaison Officer. (The addresses and telephone numbers of both are listed at the end of this book.) For the less active there is membership of one of the societies concerned with national parks and conservation, whose addresses are also listed.

But for everyone who comes to Snowdonia the best and easiest way of helping the national park to retain its beauty and character is to observe carefully the twelve requirements of the COUNTRY CODE given below:

Enjoy the countryside and respect its life and work.
Guard against risk of fire.
Fasten all gates.
Keep your dogs under close control.
Keep to public footpaths over farmland.
Use gates and stiles to cross fences, hedges, and walls.
Leave livestock, crops, and machinery alone.
Take.your litter home.
Help to keep all water clean.
Protect wildlife, plants, and trees.
Take special care on country roads.
Make no unnecessary noise.

The rowan flaunts its autumn colours below the crags of Tryfan.

Selected places of interest

The numbers after each place-name are the map grid references to help readers locate the places mentioned. Ordnance Survey maps include instructions in the use of these grid references.

ABERDYFI (SH 615960) English version of name is 'Aberdovey'. Pretty village on haven at mouth of Dyfi estuary. Once of fishing and mercantile importance, now yachting centre and holiday resort. National Park Information Centre.

BALA (SH 925360) Market town, one-time centre of wool trade. Fishing and sailing on Llyn Tegid, alongside which runs a narrow-gauge railway. Early Norman motte – with public conveniences built into it. Statue in High Street of Thomas Charles, founder of the British and Foreign Bible Society. National Park Information Centre. Market day Thursday.

BARMOUTH (SH 610160) Welsh name 'Abermaw'. Busy seaside resort with promenade and amusements. Dinas Oleu, above the town, was the first property to be acquired by the National Trust. Nearby footpath walks have grand views. Llanaber church, one and three-quarter miles north, is thirteenth century and has a fine east window.

BEDDGELERT (SH 592482) Beautifully situated village below southern heights of Snowdon. Gelert's Grave and legend make it a place of tourist pilgrimage. Riverside walks to Aberglaslyn Pass and base for ascending Moel Hebog, 2,566 ft (783 m).

BETWS-Y-COED (SH 796565) Very popular tourist centre in forested Conwy Valley, on A5 at junction of Rivers Conwy and Llugwy. Attractive shops, riverside walks. Centre for Forestry trails. National Park Visitor Centre at Y Stablau, opposite Royal Hotel, has exhibitions and slide shows.

BLAENAU FFESTINIOG (SH 700460) Slate-quarry 'capital' set in striking mountain scenery. Terminus of Ffestiniog Railway from Porthmadog and base for exploring two of the largest slate mines. Also base for visits to Tan-y-grisiau Power Station and the Llyn Stwlan Dam. National Park Information Centre.

CAERNARFON (SH 480630) Old market town outside the park, overlooking Menai Strait and dominated by the great thirteen-towered castle built by Edward I. Small picturesque port area. Segontium, on town outskirts, is an excavated Roman fort. Market day Saturday.

CONWY (SH 780775) Medieval town with its old walls complete, surrounding the fine castle (1284) at the mouth of the Conwy estuary. Small port. Plas Mawr, an Elizabethan townhouse, contains a museum. Good walks behind town, especially to the crest of Conwy mountain. Market day Tuesday.

CRICCIETH (SH 500380) Neat little seaside town with partly ruined castle on rocky mound above the sea; a Welsh castle, later rebuilt by

Edward I. Lively Fair, held annually in June, brings in country folk from miles around. Llanystumdwy, with Lloyd George's boyhood home and grave, is two miles west.

DOLGELLAU (SH 730175) Old narrow-streeted county town of Meirionnydd on the Wnion River. Above it tower the cliff-faces of Cadair Idris, which can be climbed from here. Owain Glyndŵr, last of the Welsh princes, held a Parliament here in 1400. Local walks include the long-established Torrent Walk and Precipice Walk. National Park Information Centre. Market day Friday.

HARLECH (SH 582310) The romantically sited castle built by Edward I in 1280 made this the chief town of Meirionnydd in the Middle Ages. The view of Tremadog Bay and Snowdon from the castle is renowned, as is the golf course. At the north end of the long sandy beach, which is one mile from the town, is the Morfa Harlech Nature Reserve. National Park Information Centre.

FFESTINIOG (SH 703420) Known locally as Llan Ffestiniog to distinguish it from its neighbour Blaenau Ffestiniog, this hilltop village commands a famous view and is a base for waterfall visits. Rhaeadr Cynfal is half a mile south, Rhaeadr-y-cwm three miles east, and the falls of the Goedol River one mile north west.

LLANBERIS (SH 580600) Overlooking Llyn Padarn at the foot of the Llanberis Pass and under the flank of Snowdon, this slate-quarry town has become a base for many tourist activities. The mountain railway up Snowdon starts from here. The immense underground Dinorwic Power Station can be visited (by pre-arranged tour with a conducted party) or – as a contrast – the round

keep of the thirteenth-century Dolbadarn Castle. There is a country park, two notable museums, and a narrow-gauge railway along the lakeside. National Park Information Centre.

MACHYNLLETH (SH 745010) Market town chartered in 1291, in the Dyfi Valley. Maengwyn Street has been the scene of its lively Wednesday markets for seven centuries. Owain Glyndŵr was crowned king of Wales here in 1404, probably in the building (Owain Glyndŵr Institute) which is now a museum. The Dyfi here holds salmon and the town is a centre for anglers. Nearby is the Centre for Alternative Technology with its working displays of windmills, solar-power systems and other aspects of alternative technology.

MAENTWROG (SH 665405) Small and pretty village of the Vale of Ffestiniog overlooking the Dwyryd River. The Stone (Maen) of Twrog from which it gets its name can be seen outside the west end of the little church, a four-foot sandstone pillar. Plas Tan-y-Bwlch, the Snowdonia National Park Study Centre, is half a mile east of the village and close to it are the woodlands of the Coedydd Maentwrog Nature Reserve.

PEN-Y-GWRYD (SH 660558) Famous mountain inn built 1850, overlooking the Gwynant Valley one mile east of Llanberis Pass. Birthplace of the Climbers' Club and training HQ of the successful 1953 Everest team. The 'Everest Room' of the hotel has the autographs of the Everest climbers on its ceiling.

PORTHMADOG (SH 570385) Once a thriving port for the schooners of the slate trade, now a busy market town, tourist centre, and yachting port. The harbour and the sluice-gates of W A Madocks's mile-long dam, 'The Cob', are of interest, Near the Maritime Museum the old trading-ketch *Garlandstone* is on show. The Harbour Station is the terminus of the narrow-gauge Ffestiniog Railway.

TREFRIW (SH 782632) From the eighteenth century a spa competing with Bath and Buxton, Trefriw's clients until 1939 came by paddle-steamer from Llandudno and Colwyn Bay. Today its chief interest is a woollen mill where all the process of making Welsh tweed from the raw wool to the final weaving can be seen. From Trefriw a lane climbs in three miles to Llyn Crafnant and the Cwm Glas Crafnant Nature Reserve.

Glossary

aber – river-mouth, confluence
aderyn (pl. *Adar*) – bird
afon – river
allt, gallt – height

bach, fach – small
bedd – grave
betws – chapel (bede-house)
beudy – byre, cow-house
blaen (pl. *blaenau*) – head of valley
bod – home (abode)
bont, pont – bridge
braich – arm
brith – speckled
brwynog – rushy
bryn – hill
bwlch – pass, defile
bychan – little

cadair, cader – chair
cae – field
caer – fort
canol, ganol – middle
capel – chapel
carn, carnedd – heap of stones
carreg – rock
caseg – mare
castell – castle
cau – deep hollow
cefn – ridge
celli, gelli – grove
ceunant – ravine
cidwm – wolf
cigfran, gigfran – raven
clogwyn – precipice
coch – red
coed – woodland
congl – corner
cors, gors – bog
craig – rock
crib – narrow ridge
croes – cross
cwm – cirque, valley

deg, teg – fair
dinas – fort
dol, ddol – meadow
drum – ridge
drws – door
dwr – water
dwy – two
dyffryn – valley

eglwys – church
eira – snow
esgair – shank, mountain shoulder

fach, bach – small
fawr, mawr – big
fechan – little
felin, melin – mill
ffordd – road
ffridd – mountain pasture
ffynnon – well, spring
filiast – greyhound
foel, moel – rounded hill
fraith – speckled, pied
fynydd, mynydd – mountain

gadair, gader – chair
gafr, afr – goat
gam – crooked
gigfran, cigfran – raven
glan – bank, shore
glas, las – blue or green
glyder, gludair – heap
glyn – glen
goch, coch – red
gors, cors – bog
grach – scabby
gribin – serrated ridge
grug – heather
gwastad – plain, level ground
gwern – marsh
gwrach, wrach – witch
gwyn, wyn – white
gwynt – wind

hafod, hafotty – summer dwelling
hebog – falcon
hen – old
hendre – winter dwelling
hir – long
hydd – stag

isa, isaf – lower

las, glas – green or blue
llan – church
llechog – slaty
llechwedd – hillside
llethr – slope
llithrig – slippery
lloer – moon
llwyd – grey
llwyn – grove
llyn – lake

maen (pl. *meini*) – stone
maes – field
march (pl. *meirch*) – horse
marchog – armed horseman
mawr, fawr – big
meillionen – clover
melin, felin – mill
mign, mignen – bog
mochyn (pl. *moch*) – pig
moel, foel – rounded hill
morfa – coastal marsh
mur (pl. *muriau*) – wall
mynach – monk
mynydd, fynydd – mountain

nant – brook, dingle
newydd – new

oer – cold
ogof – cave
oleu – light

pair – cauldron
pant – small hollow
pen – top, head
penrhyn – promontory
pentre, pentref – village
pistyll – spout, cataract

plas – mansion
pont, bont – bridge
pwll – pool

rhaeadr – waterfall
rhiw – hill
rhos – moorland, marsh
rhyd – ford

ucha, uchaf – upper
uwch – above

waun – moor
wen, wyn – white
wrach, gwrach – witch
wyddfa – tumulus

y (article) – the, of the
yn – in
ynys – island
ysbyty – hospice
ysfa – itching
ysgol (pl. *ysgolion*) – ladder, school
ysgubor – barn
ystrad – valley floor, strath
ystum – bend

saeth (pl. *saethau*) – arrow
sarn – paved way, causeway
sych – dry

tal – end
tan – under
tarren – hill
teg, deg – fair
tir – land
tomen – mound
traeth – stretch of shore
tre – town, hamlet
tri – three
trwyn – nose, promontory
twll – hole
ty (p. *tai*) – house
tyddyn – smallholding

Bibliography

Breeze Jones, E and Thomas,
GE *Birdwatching in Snowdonia*, John
Jones, Cardiff, 1976.
Carr, HRC and Lister, GA *The
Mountains of Snowdonia*, Crosby
Lockwood, 1948.
Condry, W *Exploring Wales*, Faber
& Faber, 1970.
Condry, W *The Snowdonia National
Park*, Collins 'New Naturalist' edition,
1966, Fontana, 1969.
Styles, S *The Mountains of North
Wales*, Gollancz, 1973.
Vale, E *The World of Wales*, Dent,
1935.

Some of these book are now out of
print but are available from public
libraries.

Useful addresses

SNOWDONIA NATIONAL PARK
Snowdonia National Park Authority
National Park Office
Penrhyndeudraeth
Gwynedd LL48 6LS
(Tel: Penrhyndeudraeth (0766)
770274)

National Park Study Centre
Plas Tan-y-Bwlch
Maentwrog
Blaenau Ffestiniog
Gwynedd LL41 3YU
(Tel: Blaenau Ffestiniog (0766) 85324)

Information Centres
Aberdyfi (0654) 472321
Bala (0678) 520367
Betws-y-Coed (06902) 665
Blaenau Ffestiniog (0766) 830360
Dolgellau (0341) 422888
Harlech (0766) 780658
Llanberis (0286) 870636

Youth and Schools Liaison Service
(Tel: Penrhyndeudraeth (0766)
770274)

Lake Warden (Llyn Tegid) Bala
(Tel: Bala (0518) 7520626)

Weather Forecast
(Tel: Llanberis (0286) 870120)

CONSERVATION ORGANIZATIONS
Council for National Parks
45 Shelton Street
London WC2H 9HJ
(Tel: 01 240 3603)

Countryside Commission
Office for Wales
Ladywell House
Newtown
Powys SY16 1RD
(Tel: Newtown (0686) 26799)

National Trust
Trinity Square
Llandudno
Gwynedd LL30 2DE
(Tel: Llandudno (0492) 74421)

Nature Conservancy Council (for
permits)
Penrhos Road
Bangor
Gwynedd
(Tel: Bangor (0248) 355141)

Snowdonia Conservation Volunteers
Volunteers Organizer
Tyddyn Siarl
Ffordd yr Eglwys
Llanberis
Gwynedd
(Tel: Llanberis (0286) 872389)

Snowdonia National Park Society
Capel Curig
Gwynedd
(Tel: Capel Curig (06904) 234)

TRANSPORT
Leaflets, bus and train timetables, and
information:
Planning Department
Gwynedd County Council
Council Offices
Caernarfon
Gwynedd LL55 1SH

Bus, train and narrow-gauge railway information (also travel agent for Britain and abroad):
Ffestiniog Railway
Harbour Station
Porthmadog
Gwynedd
(Tel: Porthmadog (0766) 2340)

MOUNTAIN RESCUE
Dial 999 and ask for POLICE

GENERAL
Plas-y-Brenin (National Centre for Mountain Activities)
Capel Curig
Gwynedd LL24 0ET
(Tel: Capel Curig (06904) 214)

Index

Page numbers in *italics* refer to illustrations.